Living the Dream

Chantelle

My Story

Chantelle Houghton was born in Essex in 1983. She has worked as a model and as a Paris Hilton lookalike. Chantelle became the nation's favourite celebrity when she won *Celebrity Big Brother* in January 2006 as the only non-celebrity housemate. It was while in the house that she met and fell in love with Preston. They got married in August 2006, and now live in Hove.

Living the Dream

Chantelle

My Story

arrow books

Published in the United Kingdom by Arrow Books in 2007

1 3 5 7 9 10 8 6 4 2

This book is a work of non-fiction based on the life, experiences and
recollections of Chantelle Houghton. In some limited cases names of people,
places, dates, sequences or the detail of events have been changed solely to
protect the privacy of others. The author has stated to the publishers that,
except in such minor respects not affecting the substantial accuracy of the
work, the contents of this book are true.

First published in the United Kingdom in 2006 by Century

Arrow Books
The Random House Group Limited
20 Vauxhall Bridge Road, London, SW1V 2SA

Addresses for companies within The Random House Group Limited can be
found at: www.randomhouse.co.uk/offices.htm

The Random House Group Limited Reg. No. 954009

A CIP catalogue record for this book
is available from the British Library

ISBN 9780099505587

The Random House Group Limited makes every effort to ensure that the papers
used in its books are made from trees that have been legally sourced from well-
managed and credibly certified forests. Our paper procurement policy can be
found at: www.randomhouse.co.uk/paper.htm

Mixed Sources
Product group from well-managed
forests and other controlled sources
www.fsc.org Cert no. TT-COC-2139
© 1996 Forest Stewardship Council
FSC

Photo credits: Rex Features; Stuart Atkins/Rex Features; David Fisher/Rex
Features; Richard Young/Rex Features; Tony Kyriacou/Rex Features; Ciaran
McCrikland/Rex Features; Huw John/Rex Features; Rex Features; Dave
Hogan/Getty Images

Printed in the UK by CPI Bookmarque, Croydon, CR0 4TD

For my mum and dad

Acknowledgements

Firstly, thank you to my loving husband, Preston.

Two people I would like to say a huge thank you to – Sharon Powers and Phil Edgar-Jones, who gave me 'that chance'. It took me five years to get it and it may never have happened, I will be eternally grateful to you both.

Thank you to John Noel, Sally Andrews and Katherine Lister for taking me under your wings and helping me with my career, my success and my personal life at times too!

To my brother Gregg for helping me, looking out for me . . . and for putting up with me over the years.

To my dad for your help and support and believing in me.

Thank you to Dean for looking after my mum while I was in *Big Brother* and encouraging me to 'Live the dream!'

To Jean Ritchie for helping me write this book, I couldn't have done it without you. It must be hard to listen to someone talking about themselves the whole time, you were very patient!

Lastly, thank you to Hannah Black and everyone at Century for their support and guidance with the making of this book.

Contents

Introduction

I paused at the top of the steps leading from the *Big Brother* house, nervously pushing my fingers through my hair. Behind me, there was an eerie quietness, a deserted house which for three weeks had been home not just to me but to nine others, all of them well-known celebrities. The disembodied voice of Big Brother broke the silence:

'Chantelle, you have won *Celebrity Big Brother*. Please leave the *Big Brother* house.'

The doors slid open – and the world went mad. The noise of thousands of people cheering was deafening. Flashbulbs were popping, and fireworks whooshed upwards, cascading light across the black January sky. Below me was a sea of shouting, screaming faces, and coming towards me was Davina McCall, with two burly security men behind her.

I walked down the steps in an excited daze. I can't even

remember getting down them, but I remember Davina clutching me and whispering, 'Well done, well done, enjoy it,' into my ear as she took me along the walkway to face the massed ranks of photographers.

I've seen the video replay and my face says it all: I was beaming from ear to ear. I smiled and laughed so much that night that my jaw ached the next day. It was the wildest, sweetest, most wonderful night anyone can imagine.

I still don't know how it happened. Me, a nobody, had won *Celebrity Big Brother*. Me, who had 8p in my bank account, had spent three weeks living alongside big names and famous faces, and somehow – I don't know how – I had walked out as the winner.

For me, just getting into the house had been a huge achievement. Every day I managed to stay in there was another victory. I'd have felt I was a winner if I had been booted out after four days. Instead, I had gone the whole way, and the British public had voted in their millions to keep me there.

It was all a dream. But it was a dream I had had for years, and now it had come true. I felt like a fairy-tale princess, as I turned and posed for the cameras. The next day, pictures of me in my short champagne-coloured dress, bought specially for this moment, and my long blonde hair extensions would be plastered across the front pages of every newspaper in the country, and my name, Chantelle, would be on so many lips.

The lights from the exploding flashguns blinded me, and as Davina whisked me away from the photographers it took me a few seconds to be able to focus my eyes again.

But then I saw my mum, with my stepdad, my dad and my best friend, crowded at the edge of the walkway, shouting my name for all they were worth.

'I love you,' I managed to yell before Davina took me to the stage where she interviewed me. Behind me were all my housemates, including Preston, who had been my friend and soulmate for the whole three weeks, and is now so much more to me.

I hardly had time to wave to them all before Davina started to question me. She offered me a pashmina – apparently the temperature was sub-zero – and all around me people were wearing fur coats, puffa jackets, hats and scarves. I had my sleeveless skinny little dress, but I didn't feel cold at all. All I could feel was excitement and happiness, and that was enough to keep me warm.

When Davina asked me why I thought I had won *Big Brother*, I truthfully had no idea. In the minutes since my win had been announced, I had not been able to think straight to work out any reasons or theories, but I answered:

'Because I'm down to earth and easy-going.'

Davina said yes, it was for those reasons, but also because I was very brave, to have taken on the task of convincing real celebrities that I, too, was a celebrity.

When she asked me what I was going to do next I was completely lost for an answer. I had no idea. What do you do, when you are a non-celebrity who has suddenly become one of the most famous faces in the land? I turned to Mum, in the audience.

'Mum, what am I going to do next?' I shouted.

'LIVE THE DREAM!' she yelled to me.

And that's just what I have been doing, living my dream. I have had a wonderful time since that night. I have had my own television show, I have been featured in countless magazines, and, most important of all, I have found true love and happiness with Preston. The whole nation saw me falling in love with him, but it was a love that seemed destined to remain unfulfilled. Now, thank goodness, we are able to be together, and our wedding was the most amazing day of my life, better even than winning *Celebrity Big Brother*.

I have met so many people, even Prince Charles. But perhaps the most touching are the little girls who shyly ask for my autograph and tell me that I am their inspiration. Me – an inspiration to others! It has all meant so much to me, the whole roller-coaster story of my time in the house, the exciting months afterwards, and the story of how I managed to get there, that I want to share it with you.

This book is the story of me Living the Dream. And what I want to say to you, every one of you who picks it up and reads it, is that you, too, can live your own dreams. Don't let anyone put you off. Just go for it, keep determined: Live the Dream.

Chapter One

Early Childhood

I was born on 21 August 1983, and from my very first breath I made sure everyone around me took notice. My mum tells me that if I had been her first baby, she would probably never have had another one. I was so demanding that for the week after Mum brought me home from hospital, my nan hardly ever put me down.

My name, Chantelle, is French and, although it isn't a real word, it comes from the French '*chanter*', which means to sing. Funny that I'm not a good singer – as you will know if you watched me singing 'I Want It Right Now' on *Celebrity Big Brother*! And the noise I made in those early days wasn't a bit tuneful, either. The minute I wasn't in someone's arms, I was yelling.

Luckily my brother Gregg, who is two and a half years older than me, was a placid baby. If he'd been like me, Mum might never have had me!

I was born at one o'clock in the morning, and it was a whirlwind delivery – Mum was only in labour for an hour, and she got to hospital just fifteen minutes before I hurtled out, apparently making enough noise to let everyone know I'd arrived.

Mum picked on my unusual name when she and Dad were visiting some friends in Belgium. They'd got to know Stephan and Cathy (pronounced 'Catty', the French way) when they were on holiday in Greece a few years earlier. Stephan worked at the holiday resort, organising sports activities. They all became good friends, and visited each other for years afterwards. Stephan and Cathy are godparents to me and Gregg.

It was while she was pregnant with me that Mum and Dad were staying with them, and Mum heard Cathy turn to a friend of hers and call her by her name, Chantal. 'If this baby is a girl,' Mum said to Dad, 'that's what we'll call her.' Not that she expected me to be a girl: she was sure she was going to have another boy. But when I popped out, the name seemed to fit – except that Mum had changed it to Chantelle, probably because she hadn't heard it properly. I'm glad, I like it better than Chantal.

It's good having an unusual name. Strangely, there was a girl who lived near us when I was little who was also called Chantelle: she was born a couple of weeks after me, and the midwife was so surprised to hear the name twice, she told Mum. At one point we were both in the same school, but never in the same class.

I was born and grew up in Wickford, in Essex. I've heard all the jokes about Essex girls, and they don't bother me – except to say that they're not true! Well, not all of them . . .

Mum and Dad are both Londoners: Mum comes originally from Bethnal Green and Dad from Peckham. They met on holiday in Spain. Mum was seventeen, and had gone away with her friend Jackie and Jackie's parents to Lloret de Mar on the Costa Brava, which was *the* place to go in those days. Two days before the end of the holiday they were sitting around the hotel pool when Jackie spotted a boy she knew from home. She started chatting to him, and he introduced them to his mate Alan. Mum really got on with him, but as she and Jackie's family were flying home two days later, she didn't expect to see him again. She told herself it was just a holiday romance, and she should forget him. But when he got home, Dad rang her – and that was it. Two years later they were married, when Mum was nineteen and Dad was twenty-two.

Dad was already a taxi driver in London. He has now been driving a black cab for over thirty years. Mum, whose name is Vivien, was working as a secretary in a solicitor's office. Their first home together was a bungalow on Canvey Island, not far from where Nan and Grandad, my mum's parents, live. But before Gregg and I came along they moved to Wickford. They liked the fact that it's a small town, and they thought it would be a good place to bring up a family.

I'm very attached to it: I'll always be a Wickford girl, wherever I live. I think I'm the only famous person ever to come from Wickford – at least, everyone tells me I've put it on the map. I read somewhere that Alvin Stardust's mum used to run a café in the town, but that's not exactly a big claim to fame.

The first house we lived in, and where I spent the first few years of my childhood, was a three-bedroomed semi in Hendon Close. When Mum had us she gave up work until we were both older – just as well, as by all accounts I was a full-time job.

I kept up my noisy act all the time I was a baby. I screamed so much that I tired myself out, and then I would be falling asleep as Mum tried to feed me. Sometimes one feed just merged into another, broken up only by bouts of me yelling. Mum was ragged with tiredness herself. Poor old Gregg couldn't work out why Mum hardly ever took him out any more – she was too busy just trying to cope with me. When we did go out shopping, I would scream all the way round the supermarket. Mum was so embarrassed: she thought people were looking at her and saying, 'That woman doesn't feed that baby,' or, worse, thinking she was a cruel mother. When she managed to take Gregg to playgroup, she'd hurry home with me, worried that I'd wake up and start my usual racket.

But as soon as I could sit up and watch the world around me, I calmed down. And once I began to be able to move about under my own steam, I became a happy, quiet (well, quieter) toddler. Sometimes I was so quiet the grown-ups didn't know what I was up to, like the time I crawled under my nan and grandad's mahogany table, one of their favourite pieces of furniture, and started to gnaw on one of the legs. Grandad noticed there was a little row of teeth-marks in the polished wood.

This is actually my earliest memory, because I can remember the sensation of my teeth sinking into the wood, and me biting harder and harder on it. Grandad later sanded it down and stained and polished it, but it never looked quite right: it still bears the scars of my baby teeth. Of course, I'm sorry that I damaged Nan and Grandad's table, but I think it proves I've got taste: I didn't chew on any old bit of laminated chipboard, I went straight for the good wood!

At our own home Dad had to take up DIY to protect me. The banister ran along the landing, and had open slats. One day when Mum had to pop down to the kitchen she left me upstairs, with a stairgate to stop me falling down. When she came back she looked up the stairwell to see my legs dangling from the landing. I'd tried to wriggle through the slats, and it was only my bulky nappy that was stopping me from falling. I was calling for Mum, but I was apparently quite happy – just determined to get downstairs somehow. Mum dashed up, taking two stairs at a time, and pulled me back through the slats. Looking back, she says she wishes she had taken a picture because I looked so funny, but at the time all she could think about was rescuing me. So Dad had to get to work to board in the banisters.

With Dad being a taxi driver, whenever we went out as a family it was in the cab. Gregg and I both used to fall asleep with our bottoms on the armrest, holding the grip rail and facing sideways. It doesn't look a very comfortable position, but apparently we could both sleep quite soundly sitting up and holding on. Really weird. It was probably the vibration of the cab that sent us to sleep.

I was never a tomboy, I always liked pretty clothes, and my favourite toys were my Barbies. I had a whole box full of different outfits for them. I was a real mummy's girl. I loved watching my mum with her rollers in, doing her make-up. She sometimes used to put a little bit of lipstick on me, and I felt really special. Mum is stunning, and looks much younger than her age. She's slim, with shoulder-length light brown hair. Dad is forever being told he looks like Mel Gibson, and he does.

I didn't do rough or boisterous games – although Gregg and I would have pretend wrestling matches, sometimes lasting for hours. We'd even have 'water breaks' to get ourselves a drink, and then carry on. I don't ever remember arguing seriously with Gregg, we got along well. Mum will tell you that we had our moments, but all kids do. He used to call me 'Splodge-oh' because I was quite chubby when I was really little. I called him 'De' before I learned to talk properly – it was my attempt at 'Gregg'.

Other favourite toys were Bert and Ernie, two of the characters from *Sesame Street*. They were really Gregg's, but we'd take one each and have play-fights with them. I didn't have a great collection of stuffed toys, but I did have a purple and white dog, which I just called Fluffalump, because that was the name of the range of toys.

One Christmas I remember waking up really early, and seeing the pile of presents at the bottom of my bed. I went into Gregg's room, and it seemed to me that his pile was bigger. So I was going to change them all over. But luckily I didn't: I'm not sure that I would have wanted a football strip, and he certainly wouldn't have been very keen on Barbie's accessories!

Most of all, we liked playing with Boycey, our dog. We got him as a puppy when I was four and a half years old. He was a Staffordshire bull terrier, and he was just perfect. We collected him on a Sunday, and brought him home in a cardboard box. He sat next to the warm cooker, shivering – he was probably terrified, with everyone cooing over him and two little children wanting to play with him. He was so tiny he sat in Mum's hand. He was brindle-coloured, with a flash of white fur down his chest. I remember one of my cousins asking Mum: 'Why has Boycey got cream all down his chest?'

Me and Gregg used to tease him by dangling Bert and Ernie off pieces of string over the banisters, and he used to jump to try to get them. When he was really little I used to put dolls' dresses on him, and Gregg would put an Arsenal shirt on him – it had to be Arsenal! Boycey didn't mind being pulled about. When there was snow we'd wrap him in a blanket and take him outside. Dad bought a stripy tank top for him for the bad weather, and he wore it a lot the first winter we had him – the sleeves holes were so tight they rubbed the hair off his little legs, which we didn't realise until later.

Dad would take us out for walks with him, and Boycey would always have a stick in his mouth. Every morning, when Dad went to the shop for his paper, Boycey would carry it back. Sometimes he even went to work with Dad, sitting in the front of the cab. He just loved being with people.

Everyone thinks Boycey got his name from the character in *Only Fools and Horses*, but that's not how he came by it. We called him Rocky when we first had him, but Dad would always call him 'Boy'. Me and Gregg changed that to Boycey, and before long that was his name. He learned it quickly enough, and never seemed confused about the change.

From the age of about five I went to dancing classes – tap and ballet. Mum used to buy me lovely little tutus, which I loved so much I wanted to wear them all the time. Years later, when we were in the *Celebrity Big Brother* house, Pete Burns really laid into Traci Bingham for saying that she 'loved' certain shoes or outfits. He said the word should have been 'liked', and that you can't 'love' shoes and dresses. Well, Pete, I beg to differ. Although the love you feel for certain outfits is not the same, obviously, as the love you feel for another human being or even a pet, it's definitely stronger than 'like'. Pete, of all people, loves his clothes. And I have always loved mine, even as a small child.

When I was little Mum kept my hair long – it was dark brown, its natural colour (I take after my dad) – and I loved her dressing it up with ribbons, pretty slides and scrunchies. I was very patient when she brushed it and plaited it, or put it into bunches, French plaits or a ponytail. I was happy to let her spend ages doing it, even when I was quite small. Actually, she was more or less forced to let it grow long, because the first time she took me to the hairdresser's to get it trimmed, when I was about eighteen months old, I threw a tantrum and arched my body so that my legs wouldn't bend to put me in the chair, and Mum had to give up. Funny, when you think I really like having my hair done now.

But one of my earliest memories is about my hair, and it's not a happy one. I remember being called to the front of the class in infants school, and the teacher looked down at me, then told me to come outside with her. She checked my hair and told me I had head lice. I started to cry, and I just didn't stop. Mum had to come and get me, and I cried all the way to the chemist where we bought that horrible smelly stuff you have to plaster on to get rid of them. I was secretly glad to be out of school for the day, but I was mortified at the idea of having nits.

One of the first ever dance routines I performed in public was on the big stage at the Victoria Palace Theatre in Southend, about twelve miles away from Wickford. All the girls from my dancing class were playing little mice. My nan is good with a needle, and she made my costume. Mum has a video of it, and there I am, even at that age, leading the others and pulling another girl back into the right place. Apparently I was always the leader. Mum says I was naturally confident and didn't seem to suffer from nerves – I still very rarely get nervous. I think it's that trait, as much as any, that helped me get through three weeks in a house full of famous people!

When I was about seven I joined Wickford Majorettes, which meant going every Monday evening to a local hall to drill our routines. It was great fun, but also hard work. Mum and me would practise my routines, up and down the living room, on Saturday afternoons and when Dad came home the place would be full of pompoms and my little outfit, which was a white pleated skirt, a short double-breasted red jacket in a military style, white socks and white shoes. Mum was forever whitening the shoes, which had to be immaculate.

We'd take part in parades, and put on shows at carnivals. We once marched seven miles in a parade, batons twirling and pompoms shaking all the way. It was in summer, a really hot day, and one girl fainted from the heat. Mum always came with me, she never wanted me to travel on the bus with the older girls. She and another mum would take it in turn to drive us. Mum has always been my best friend.

When I was eight I won the Majorette of the Year award. We were supposed to do three routines one with baton twirling, one with pompoms, and another one, but I only did the first two, as I hadn't practised the third. I came first in the baton twirling and second in the pompoms, and my overall score was high enough for me to take the top prize. Mum is a much shyer person than me, and she was always amazed that I could perform onstage in front of a hall full of people without any worries. I never worried about people watching me, as long as I had had time to practise. After all, an audience is just made up of individual people.

Saturdays were always a very special time for me and Mum. We would go shopping, getting the week's food but also wandering around looking at clothes, which we both love, and then afterwards we would go to visit Nan and Grandad. When he was really young Gregg would come too, but he doesn't have the shopping gene like me and

Mum, and as soon as he was old enough he decided he'd rather be with his mates kicking a football around.

I loved the shopping trips, and I usually managed to persuade Mum to buy me something, even if it was only a new hair ribbon. When we got to Nan's she would say to Mum: 'And what have you bought her this week?' I don't think I was spoiled, because I certainly couldn't have everything I wanted. Mum brought me up to understand the value of money – to this day, I think it is ridiculous to pay thousands of pounds for a designer dress, especially if it can only be worn once at some glamorous event. Not that I don't like spending money on clothes – I love it, and I know I spend too much. But I'd rather have lots of cheaper outfits than one designer one.

When we got to Nan and Grandad's house I always got a little bit of spoiling. Grandad would give me my weekly £1 spending money, and he'd walk me to the local shop to buy some chocolate, or he'd have chocolate in a drawer for me. I saw my other grandparents, on Dad's side, too, but never as much, as they lived in London.

I've always enjoyed shopping with Mum, I still do. I didn't even mind going round Tesco buying food, which lots of kids would have found boring. I remember one Friday night, when I persuaded Mum and Dad to take me to the café in Tesco. The store had a 'bottomless cup' offer, which meant they would keep filling up your drink. I desperately wanted to go, so there we were at eleven o'clock on a Friday night, me drinking hot chocolate. It was so exciting to be out late, in the dark. I thought it was such a wonderful treat.

On Sundays we'd all go to football. Dad was coaching a team that Gregg played for, and from being very young I can remember standing on the touchline with Mum, watching them. Then we'd go home for Sunday dinner, which wasn't always a traditional roast – Mum makes great rogan josh curry, which we all love.

We'd have family outings to McDonald's or a pizza restaurant. And at weekends in the summer Dad would drive us to Southend or the beach at Canvey Island. Boycey loved swimming in the sea, so Dad would throw balls and sticks for him. Then we'd get lunch at the little cafés along the beach.

The best holiday I'd ever had – until I went to Morocco with Preston – was a trip to Disneyland in Florida, when I was nine. Mum, Nan, Gregg and me went – I think Dad was too busy working. I know I cried almost the whole way there on the plane, sobbing my heart out, because he wasn't with us. But – sorry Dad! – I soon forgot to be unhappy when we got there. It was the best time ever.

I went to Wickford County Junior School, which was just round the corner from where we lived. I was very happy there, and had lots of friends. I even loved the uniform, which was a grey skirt, white shirt and a green cardigan. In the summer we wore green candy-striped dresses, which looked really cute. My favourite teacher was Miss Bridgewater, who was kind and friendly, and also young and pretty with lovely blonde hair. See, I loved long blonde hair, even then!

When I was seven, we moved to another house, even nearer to the school, and with a big river just a stone's throw away. My bedroom was painted blue, which I didn't like – I've always loved pink. Mum is good at decorating, and she changed it to pink for me. At first I had the same white bedroom furniture I'd had at the other house, but later on we had fitted wardrobes built. It's still my bedroom to this day, even though I don't live there any more, and I feel really secure and happy whenever I'm there.

My best friend was Danielle, who only joined the school in our last year there, when I was ten. She came to live six doors away from us, and from the moment we knew each other, we became inseparable. We did everything together. We both loved *The Sound of Music* film, and Danielle had a dressing-up box, so we'd put these long dresses on and go dancing up and down the pavement as if we were running over the hills with the von Trapp family. The riverbank was very near to our road, so we'd go down there and run up and down the banks. And, although she wasn't a majorette, she'd help me practise my routines.

We used to play a game in her bedroom, which we'd seen some girls doing in a film (I can't remember its name). We'd close our eyes and have to make our way round the room above the ground, stepping from a chair to a table, to the wardrobe and the bed, without touching the floor.

Only the other day I heard the All Saints song 'I Know Where It's At' on the radio – and I instantly knew where I was when that record came out. I was back with Danielle, dancing around to it, singing the words.

At school in the lunch breaks we'd go out on the playing field, and the girls would all be doing the 'crab', which is when you bend over backwards and put your hands down on the floor. You need someone to watch, just in case you topple over. I tried to do it at home once, and I fell over on to the wooden floor and really smashed my face down hard. The colour drained from my lips and I could hardly talk.

In our final weeks at junior school we put on a show. It was *We'll Meet Again*, and it had all the old Second World War numbers in it. I had a really cute dress, and Mum did my hair with a big curl, and I wore bright red lipstick. We learned how to jitterbug, and Mum remembers that I was at the front of the stage, really confident, dancing away in front of an audience.

Being at junior school was a happy time, I can't remember ever being miserable. In fact, my whole childhood up to this point was idyllic, and it's all down to my mum, so I'm really grateful. I know how lucky I was to have her and Dad.

Chapter Two

The Bullies

It started with hair pulling and whispered name-calling. It ended with a full-scale attack – five girls on to me. It was a horrible few months, and it has left its mark on me. I don't regret it happening because I believe the whole experience made me stronger, more self-reliant, more determined to make something of my life to prove to the bullies I'm somebody to be reckoned with. But that doesn't mean that I think bullying is ever a good thing, and that's why I was really happy to be asked to take part in the Bully Watch London campaign, organised by the charity Beatbullying, soon after I came out of the *Celebrity Big Brother* house.

My problems started when I was twelve, and in my second year at Bromfords Senior School, our local comprehensive. I was standing in the tuck-shop queue, and I had a big spot on my nose. As you can guess, I was very self-conscious about it. I didn't normally have a spot problem, probably because of the really healthy diet Mum laid on, with loads of vegetables and fruit.

So I was upset about it anyway, without anyone saying anything. But then this group of girls, from the year above me, started taking the mick:

'What's that she's got growing on her face?'

'Eugggh, yuk, she's got a growth on her face.'

They went on and on, and I went bright red and there were tears running down my cheeks.

'If I've still got this spot tomorrow, I'm not coming into school. I'm staying home,' I told Danielle.

Sure enough, the spot was still there in the morning and I ended up staying at home for the rest of the week. Mum completely understood, and she was happy to let me stay home until the spot cleared up.

The spot may have gone, but the trouble hadn't. When I got back to school, those girls started to pick on me at every opportunity. They would pull my hair, try to grab my school bag, whisper horrible names. I used to plan my route around the school, from lesson to lesson, trying my best to avoid them. I stopped going to the tuck shop, in case they were hanging around there. And at the end of the day, instead of chatting to my friends, I'd get away as fast as I could. I just didn't want to see them.

I'd been going to a school gymnastics club, but I stopped that because they were there. I don't know why they chose me to be their target, but for some reason they made me the object of all their nastiness. They were bigger than me, there was a whole group of them, and I was terrified.

I didn't know what to do. Mum was very worried about

me: she says that I changed in a few days from being my normal, cheerful, sunny self to being morose and tearful. We talked about her coming up to the school, but we could see it might make matters worse.

I stayed home a great deal. I'd set off walking to school with Dad, who was going to the shop for his paper, and then I'd burst into tears, and I'd be crying so much he'd let me go back home. He couldn't force me to go when it was making me so unhappy: I don't think any loving parent could force a child to go if they were in that state. So I guess I missed a lot of my education, thanks to the bullies.

When I did go, my life was hell. I think the bullies were always really pleased to discover I was in school, so that they could have fun taunting me and frightening me. They'd say things about my spot, or they'd just whisper about me, staring at me so that I knew they were talking about me. The spot thing went on for ages. A gang of girls walking towards you down a corridor is very intimidating. They used to barge into me. Once one of them shouted 'Whore!' at me, and I had no idea what it meant, and I retorted by saying 'Pig!' I asked Mum that night what 'whore' meant, and I was shocked when she told me. One day, things got so bad that I broke down in tears and rang Mum. She decided that it had gone too far, so she came up to the school and together we saw one of the senior staff, a man. We sat in a lobby, the three of us round a table, trying to explain what had been going on and why I was upset.

The result was very disappointing. I think the teacher was relieved that nothing more serious, like physical injury, had happened. And as for the girls who were doing the bullying, they made it obvious that they knew I was there by walking around near us the whole time, grinning and even waving at me. It would have been difficult for that teacher not to have known what was happening, yet he seemed to ignore their behaviour. I got the impression that he was as anxious to avoid confrontation as I was.

Mum got the same impression. At the end of the meeting we were told that everything would be sorted. But as we walked away from the school we both felt that nothing had been resolved, and I was just as scared of the bullies as I had ever been.

But something did change, and very soon afterwards. It was break time, and I'd been chatting with my friends. I can't remember what we were talking about, but, knowing us, it would probably have been make-up, clothes or music. Those were our favourite topics. Anyway, towards the end of break, just before the bell went to tell us we had to go to lessons, I decided to go to the toilet. When I came out, the corridors were deserted as everyone had made their way to the classrooms. I was walking up an empty corridor, and went past an intersection with another corridor on my left, and passed a window into a classroom.

I didn't turn and look to my left, in the door of the classroom. I just carried on walking, hurrying because I was late. Suddenly, I was attacked from behind. Someone grabbed my hair, jerking my head back hard. I cried out in shock, and spun round. I was face to face with the main bully, the ringleader of the gang. Behind her were the four other girls, all laughing and jeering at me. They had seen me from the classroom.

I don't know what happened inside me, but something snapped. I'd had enough. I wasn't going to run away any more. I lashed out at her, and we started fighting. The others joined in, but I was furious and I was really going for it, punching and kicking for all I was worth. I don't think I'd ever realised how much of a temper I have when I'm provoked. The bullies didn't know either. The girl reeled back and I managed to break away, running down the corridor crying. I ran out of school and rang for Mum.

I'd never had a fight before, and I was shaking. I didn't go back to school until the next week, but standing up to them made the difference, completely. It turned everything round. They didn't bother me any more, not even the slightest snigger at me. I walked past them, and they said nothing. One of them actually stopped me in the corridor and said, 'It wasn't me started on you.'

I don't condone using violence to tackle bullying, I know it is the wrong approach. I just saw red and fought back, but it's not the best solution, and it could have made things worse.

The best bit for me was that a boy in my year, Steven Johnson, saw the fight because he was also late for his lesson. 'God,' he said to me afterwards, 'I wouldn't like to get on the wrong side of you.' That really cheered me up.

(A couple of years later Steven said to me: 'I can just picture you when you're grown up, you'll be like a TV or movie star or something, with your mobile phone glued to your ear.' If you are reading this, Steven, I don't know if you remember making that prediction – but you got close to it, didn't you?)

I've never seen the girls who bullied me since they left school. But since I've been famous a man came up to me in the street and said he knew a friend of mine. He mentioned her name, and said she wanted to say hello to me. She was one of the gang who bullied me. I simply said:

'I'm sorry, but I don't know who you mean. I don't know anybody of that name.'

It was quite ridiculous for her to claim she'd been a friend of mine.

It was two weeks after my eleventh birthday when I started at Bromfords. When I arrived on my first day I found I had been put into the top stream. That should have been good news, but for me it wasn't: none of the other girls from my junior school were in the same class as me.

I really missed my friends, and the other girls in my class all seemed to know each other. I felt miserable and left out. I could see my friends at lunchtime and at breaks, but had to go off without them afterwards. I moaned about it so much that in the end Mum decided I would be happier if I was moved to a lower stream.

Looking back, it sounds quite mad to ask to be put down, but I just wasn't happy. Mum tried to persuade me to wait a while, to see if I could make new friends, but every day was misery for me and going to school was an ordeal. I was so unhappy I couldn't concentrate in class, and I stopped doing my homework.

When Mum came up to the school to explain the situation, the Head of Year also tried to persuade me to give it a bit more time. Finally, though, they all accepted that it was more important for me to be happy than anything else, and I was moved to a lower stream. I had been in the school for less than half a term when I moved forms.

I was back with Danielle, who was my best friend, and the other girls I knew. I floated through school after that (until the bullying). I wasn't one of the really popular girls, and I wasn't in any particular group, but I got on with all of them. Our uniform was navy blue: we wore trousers and a blazer, with a white shirt and a navy tie with light blue stripes. I didn't rebel against the uniform because I quite liked it. But I wore ridiculously high shoes, which I would never wear today. They were disgusting. They had platform soles and thick heels, and made me even taller than I am. I'm five feet seven inches now, and I was always one of the tallest girls at school.

I didn't need one of those intense friendships that some girls have, because my closest friend has always been my mum, completely. Even now, I phone her about ten times a day. She's been a terrific mum to me and Gregg. By the time we were at senior school she was working again, at first as a legal secretary in London, and then with a firm of solicitors in Wickford. Every day she would ring us five minutes after we were due to get home from school, to make sure we were there. If she ever popped out from home, she would always leave us a note saying where she was and when she would be back. She was definitely a very hands-on mum.

I have always been able to say anything to her. She

would never be shocked or disapproving of anything, and I know I can completely rely on her.

I can't honestly say I liked lessons at school – well, not most of them. In fact, my favourite thing at school was definitely the bell that said the day was over and we could go home. But I was good at English, which I enjoyed, and I also liked cookery. I still enjoy cooking – Preston says I'm a genius cook! But I don't think my family ever felt tempted by the dishes I made at school. I can remember taking home a pizza which had gone really soggy. Gregg wouldn't eat it, and I think even Boycey turned his nose up at it.

Mum did the cooking at home, and I was allowed to help out. She made sure we ate very healthily: we never had burger-and-chips-type meals. Every three months or so we were allowed to have chips, for special occasions. I have been vegetarian since I was eleven, when I happened to see a documentary which showed how burgers and sausages are made. It completely put me off. I sometimes wish I hadn't seen it, because I find life as a vegetarian quite difficult. I have to make sure I get enough protein, which isn't easy because I don't eat cheese. But whenever I think of the way animals are farmed, or what goes into burgers and sausages, I know I just can't go back to eating meat. I don't generally eat fish, either, although I do have salmon and cod occasionally.

I gave up cheese after I started to get terrible migraines, when I was about thirteen. If you've never had a migraine, don't let anyone try to tell you it's just a bad headache. It is much, much worse. The first sign for me that one is coming is when my eyes start to go weird, and when I look at someone I can only see one of their eyes, or if I look at a book or magazine the words just swim. Then the pain starts, a real splitting pain that is off the scale, and which doesn't go away when you take painkillers. It is bad enough to make you vomit, and the only help is to lie down in a dark room.

I can remember a migraine coming on while I was in a maths lesson, and the teacher wouldn't let me leave the room. My eyes were cloudy, I couldn't see the writing on the book I was supposed to be working on, I couldn't see anything written on the blackboard, and the pain was excruciating, so bad that I cried all through the lesson.

When I saw the doctor he said there are three things that commonly cause migraines: cheese, oranges and chocolate. So I gave them all up, instantly, and I have been free of migraines for several years, touch wood. After a while I started eating chocolate again, and the first time I was worried that it might bring the problem back. But, thank goodness, it never has: I'd really hate to be deprived of chocolate for the rest of my life!

I've never experimented with reintroducing oranges or cheese. I'm sure cheese is a trigger for me, because I'd eaten pizza for lunch the day I had the migraine in the maths lesson.

I do eat eggs nowadays, but never on their own – they have to be cooked as part of something. For instance, I will eat egg pasta, and biscuits and cakes that have egg in them. But I won't eat a boiled or fried egg. I don't know why not – I just went off them at the same time that I stopped eating meat. At first I wouldn't eat anything that even had a trace of egg in it. I can remember Mum was going to cook some pasta and I kept saying, 'Has it got eggs in it?'

'No, no eggs,' Mum said, and she reeled off the list of ingredients. But she kept her thumb on the packet, and I insisted she move it. Of course, the word 'egg' was underneath, so I wouldn't eat it. It must have been a real pain, finding things that I could and would eat. It's still difficult, but at least I'm old enough to buy and cook my own food now.

Apart from the migraines, the only health problem I have had was really severe stomach pains, when I was fourteen. My stomach became very bloated and distended. Mum took me to the doctor's, and she was really shocked when he told her I might be pregnant. Of course, she knew I didn't have a boyfriend and that I couldn't possibly be having a baby, but just for a few seconds her face was a picture. I knew I couldn't be pregnant, but at the same time I was in such pain and my tummy was so swollen I began to think it was a phantom pregnancy, or that I had got pregnant from sitting on a toilet seat. I knew this was an old wives' tale and couldn't be true, but it was such a weird thing to have happened that I began to think of all sorts of explanations.

The doctor sent me for an ultrasound scan to find out what was really wrong at Basildon hospital, in the maternity unit, along with all the genuinely pregnant women. I was supposed to drink a litre of water before we went, so that my bladder would be full. But Mum and me got it wrong, and I drank three litres. When we got there

I was dying to go to the loo, but they wouldn't let me. I was so uncomfortable that I was sitting on the edge of the chair, with my legs tightly crossed. The scan found nothing, and in the end the doctor put it all down to stress. It was at the same time as the bullying, so it was probably a physical reaction to that. Mum was relieved. But I was still upset because the pain and the bloating hadn't gone away.

When I read in the newspapers of girls who get pregnant at fourteen or even younger, I feel very sad. Going into the mother and baby unit when I was so young meant that there were a few disapproving glances thrown my way, by people who obviously thought I must be pregnant to be there.

I was always into clothes, and luckily for me, my mum is very fashion-conscious. We loved looking at clothes together, and she would always buy me the latest things. We both knew how to get a look to work, even with just the cheapest accessories. A belt that is just right can transform an outfit. We would share magazines. *OK!* was our favourite, because we were both fascinated by the lives of famous people, and we loved looking at what the celebs were wearing. I can't remember when I first began to have the dream, the dream that has now become a reality for me. But I can remember always feeling that I wanted to be someone, and to have a very comfortable life. It wasn't something I thought about all the time, and I didn't plan how to make it happen, it was just a feeling that was always there. I certainly never consciously said to myself:

'I want to be famous.'

I wasn't inspired by anyone in particular, although I loved looking at what the Spice Girls were wearing. When I saw celebrities with their glamorous lives, and looking so lovely, I wanted to be like that. I didn't envy them, and I didn't want to be them: I just wanted that sort of life, with the money to make the most of my looks.

Just a few weeks ago, I was sitting outside Starbucks in Carnaby Street, and two little girls came up and said that I was their inspiration. It made me feel very emotional, because it is only a short time ago that I would go to bed and dream of being someone: now they are going to bed and dreaming of being me, and doing the sort of thing I've done.

Because I was very clued up about fashion, sometimes I would be ahead of the other girls. I can remember buying long, over-the-knee black socks and going to a school disco in them, in my first year at senior school. Mum walked me there, and we heard other kids sniggering about them. When I got to the disco, there was more pointing and laughing. I didn't care, I liked them and felt confident in them. Two weeks later, all the girls were wearing them.

That same disco was when I first had my heart broken – or so I thought at the time. I had my first boyfriend, a boy called Ricky Nunn. I was only eleven, and there was obviously nothing to it, looking back. But at the time I thought I really liked him. When the last song came on, I expected him to dance with me, and I was really excited by it. But instead he danced with another girl, and kissed her right in front of me. Four years later, when we were all leaving school, he wrote in my Leavers' Book: 'Good luck – and sorry about the Year Seven disco.'

I really enjoyed my first taste of modelling, which came when I was in my first year at senior school. There was a fashion show being put on to help raise money for the school, and a few girls were chosen as models. We had to walk up and down a proper catwalk. Some of the girls were very nervous, but I wasn't. I modelled two outfits, and I can still remember them: a little black skirt with a black-and-white check waistcoat, and a white shirt with leggings. Afterwards several other mums told my mum that I should take up modelling.

So when we saw an advert in the paper for child models, we went along to a hotel not far from where we live. Mum had to pay £30 for them to take some photos of me. They said that they would either ring up to put me on the books of the model agency or, if I was unsuccessful, they would send us the photos. We never heard from them. I was so disappointed: I'd been very excited about it. Dad even went round to the address they had given for the agency in London, but it didn't exist. He drove up and down the street until he found the right number, but when he went into the building nobody had ever heard of the company. That was my first taste of how difficult it is to launch a modelling career, and how careful you have to be. It's disgusting that people will make money out of kids' dreams.

But it didn't stop me dreaming of being a model. Me and Danielle used to take pictures of each other, trying to pose like we were professional models.

My first paid work started at thirteen. I really wanted to earn some money, to buy magazines and hair accessories and things like that. So I signed up to deliver a local free newspaper every Thursday. Of course, Mum didn't want me walking around the town on my own, particularly in the winter when it was dark by the time I came home from school. So she always came with me, and sometimes, if I had a lot of homework or whatever, she would do the deliveries for me. It became Mum's paper round. Aren't I lucky to have a mum like that? I hated doing it. It cast a shadow over the whole day on Thursday, knowing I was going to have to do it, and it only earned me about £4.50, although it could be more if there were a lot of leaflets to go out with the papers.

But I liked spending the money. I didn't get regular pocket money, but Mum gave us money for school every day, to buy lunch, and if I was going out with my friends she'd give me more. When we were old enough, I'd go with my friends to Basildon on Saturdays or during school holidays, to wander around the shops. We were all really interested in clothes, but because we didn't have much money to spend we had to be very picky about what we bought. We could spend a whole day wandering around, without buying anything.

When I was fourteen, me and my friend spotted a good way to make a bit of money. Dad is a qualified football coach, and he was managing the Basildon United youth team. Gregg played for the team, and Mum was secretary. We used to go on a Sunday morning to watch them play.

There was a bar at the club, but there was nowhere anyone could get a cup of tea or coffee. We spotted a caravan with a hatch that was just standing there, so we set ourselves up in business selling teas, coffees and biscuits. With as many as sixty people attending each match, we were kept busy. We didn't make much money, but it was good experience, buying the supplies and making sure it ran smoothly.

I was always much keener on spending the money I earned on clothes than on CDs. I liked Blue, and Take That, but I was never the sort of girl to have posters of them everywhere.

Most years our family went on holiday to Benidorm, which was really cool. I love the sun, just lying on a beach or by a pool and soaking it up. Although I had a completely wicked time in the *Big Brother* house, when I watch the show in the summer and see them all sunbathing, I envy them. It was freezing cold January when I was in there, so the only tan I came out with was from a bottle.

I was fifteen when Mum and Dad split up. I know it can sometimes be very difficult for teenagers to cope with their parents divorcing and some families become divided, with lots of bitterness and anger. But I can honestly say it wasn't like that for us. Whatever unhappiness Mum and Dad felt, they managed to keep it away from me and Gregg until the end. They both put us first, and they made sure we were all right.

They married very young, and I think the relationship just ran out of steam. There were never any nasty scenes. They did all the things that a mum and dad do, and we still went out as a family, but as a couple they just weren't together for some time. The saddest thing about it for me is that they stayed together for a few years when they weren't happy, just so that me and Gregg could have a mum and a dad. They did their best not to make us feel guilty about it, but they did tell us that they had waited to split up until we were both old enough, and until the circumstances were right. They never played us off against each other, they agreed early on that we were the most important thing. I can only thank them for it from the bottom of my heart: they have both been absolutely wicked parents.

It was a relief when they split up: it meant that they both had a chance of finding happiness, which is all I could possibly wish for both of them. I think it must be more difficult for kids who have to move house or school when their parents split. If that had happened to us, I think I would have been much more traumatised. But Mum, Gregg and me stayed in the same house, and obviously I stayed at the same school and saw all the same friends.

I was at home when Dad finally decided to move out for good. I wasn't surprised, because somehow I'd suspected for a little while it was on the cards. When he actually left it was sad. Gregg and me both went outside to say goodbye, and hug and kiss him, and I cried. But I really didn't want to make it hard for him.

At first when Dad moved out he lived in London, but before long he had his own place in Wickford, so I didn't even have to go far to see him. He kept in close touch. He still came round to take Boycey out, and he went to football with Gregg on Sundays, just the same as always. It was strange not having him there at breakfast time, but apart from that it all seemed kind of normal, just that he didn't sleep at the house. He made sure Mum had the same amount of money she had always had, so in that way I didn't notice any difference. I still go round to his flat now to see him regularly and he's very much part of my life.

It was about this time that I had my first proper boyfriend. Brett was just a lad from round where we lived, and it certainly wasn't anything serious. He was the same age as me, but he went to a different school. Although I saw him for about three years, it was not a deep relationship. I wasn't in love. It's just that, at a certain time, everyone has a boyfriend and I would have felt odd without one. We would just hang out together with a crowd of other kids our age. Sometimes we'd go to the local youth club on a Wednesday night, where there would be a disco, although I would usually dance with my girlfriends. The lads would play snooker. On Friday and Saturday evenings we'd all go out for a walk, and sit in the local park, chatting and flirting, and occasionally we'd go to the cinema. We were too young to go out for a drink.

By the time we split up I wanted to move on. Girls seem to grow up faster than boys, and, even though I wasn't old enough, I wanted to start going to pubs and clubs. I don't think he was ready. It was my decision to split, but to be honest there was no great heartache for either of us. It wasn't a heavy relationship.

I was happy when it was time to leave school. I passed seven GCSEs, and lots of my friends went on to college, but I had had enough of classrooms. I wanted to earn money, and start enjoying myself. It was great to get out of school

Chapter Three

The Big Wide World

The jubilation of leaving school didn't last for long. I started work straight away – an office job with a catering company. It was in London, so I joined the throng of commuters travelling for more than an hour every morning to get to work. It wasn't in a part of London where there were shops or things to do, so I wasn't very excited by being in the big city. I was a trainee receptionist, and I found the job through an agency. I had no real idea what I wanted to do: we had some careers advice at school, but at fifteen not many people really know what they are suited for and will enjoy. My best – and favourite – subject at school was English, but that didn't exactly help me find a job.

I was only fifteen when I started work: because my birthday is in late August, I was always one of the youngest in my year at school, and I actually started work four weeks before my sixteenth birthday.

I didn't like it. It came as a shock to leave behind a world of girls my own age. I may not have enjoyed lessons much, but at least at school I was with my friends, and we could chatter at break times about make-up, hair, shoes, clothes, music, boys – all the things that girls of that age are interested in.

Suddenly I was in a world of older people, the only young one. Most of the people I worked with were friendly and tried to make me feel welcome, but I had little in common with them. And one of them, the one immediately above me who was supposed to show me what to do, was really unpleasant. She made me feel a failure if I had to ask her how to do something she had already shown me, so in the end I became afraid to ask. If I did things wrong – misfiled papers or forgot to do something – she would sigh and mutter and make me feel hopeless. But if I checked with her what I was supposed to do, she would be annoyed.

If I had nothing to do I'd ask her if there was anything I could help with, because I thought that was polite. She wouldn't even answer, or she'd be really brusque. She was, in a mild way, a workplace bully. She didn't actually set out to make my life a misery in the way the bullies at school did, but the result was the same. I dreaded going.

The others never invited me to have lunch with them, which I can totally understand because I was so much younger. So I spent my lunchtimes alone, walking the streets of London. I was hungry, but I wouldn't go into a café or a restaurant and sit on my own. So I would buy a

Me only a few days old
with Dad and Gregg.

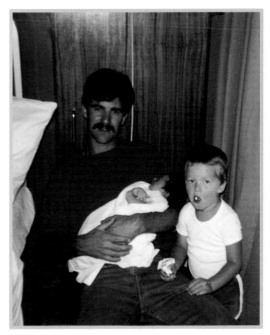

Three weeks old.

Five months old,
in my christening dress.

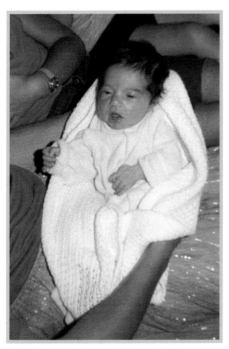

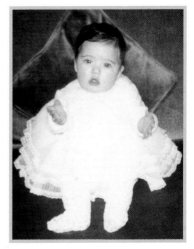

Me and my
bucket of sand
on the beach
in Spain.

Me, aged one, with Gregg in Spain.

Aged two with Gregg, aged four,
at home in Essex.

Me and Gregg
at the circus.

At a fete, aged three.

My school photo, aged four.

With Dad and Gregg
in Trafalgar Square.

Mum in
Trafalgar Square.

Aged six.

Me on the right, with Gregg and my godfather's daughter Judith at Southend airport in January 1988.

My beloved dog Boycey, wrapped up in a blanket.

My sixth birthday party in McDonalds, Essex.

Me, aged eight, as Majorette of the Year in 1991.

Cheers! Me and Dad in Spain.

Me and little Boycey!

Wickford County Junior School concert 'We'll Meet Again' on 15th December 1993.
(*Inset above*) Me, aged eleven, attempting to sing 'Somewhere Over the Rainbow'
on a family holiday in Benidorm.
(*Inset below*) A fashion show at school in October 1994.

Me and Mum at the Aquapark on holiday in Spain.

The day of my eleventh birthday
at home in Wickford.

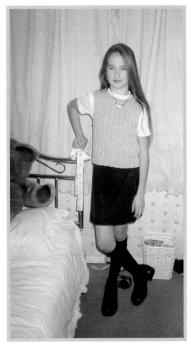

School disco night – look at
those knee-high socks!

sandwich and sit in the park trying to eat it without anyone seeing me. If it was raining I would just walk and walk. I was so lonely.

I was told when I started there that I would not be given much to do until I had learned a few things. So all I did was bind files and make tea, and I couldn't see it going anywhere. I wanted to stick it out, because I wanted to have some money, but I was very unhappy. I wasn't getting home until 6.30 p.m., which seemed to me to be very late, after years of leaving school at 3 p.m.

I was too tired to go out in the evening: all I did was have something to eat and go to bed, so that I could be up early the next day for work. I didn't have a boyfriend, and by this time my friend Danielle and her family had moved away from Wickford, so I didn't see her any more. And although I still saw my old school friends around the town we didn't really keep in touch. At weekends I would go out for a drink with my mum sometimes, but I often just stayed in. I did think sometimes that I didn't have many friends, but I suppose it didn't bother me. I had a sort of tunnel vision, wanting to do something with my life, and that was the most important thing.

After a few months I decided to leave – there were plenty of other jobs going. It was with a great feeling of relief that I handed in my notice, and served my last week there cheerfully, knowing it was all going to end very soon.

Of course, I needed to work, to earn money. But I knew that I wanted something more out of life than settling down into an office job. I couldn't say exactly what I wanted, but I was sure there was something more enjoyable, something more suited to me. And deep inside I had my dream, that one day I would be somebody, I would do something that would show everyone who had ever tried to put me down that I was worth more than they imagined.

Finding what I wanted to do was hard. My next job was with a credit-card company, not far from home, but I had to start at 6 a.m. This meant waking up at 5 a.m., and, as there was no other way of getting there, Mum would also get up and drive me there. Then she would go home and get ready to go to her own job. She was really good, but it wasn't a long-term solution. And besides, I didn't enjoy this job, either.

Most of my friends had gone to college, and I did think about training, perhaps as a beautician. But deep down I didn't want to go back to studying. There was never any pressure from Mum and Dad to go to college or get qualifications: they both just wanted me to be happy. I had maybe ten jobs in the next three years, and my CV was getting longer and longer. I reckon that every time I went for a job the employer would be thinking, 'Why has she had so many jobs? What's wrong with her?'

One job I had was as a receptionist for a transport company, and again there was a woman there who bullied me. I arrived nine minutes late one day, and she went ballistic. She was a complete bitch who made my life hell. She never said 'please' or 'thank you' – and you will know, if you saw my outburst about Dennis Rodman when we were in the *Celebrity Big Brother* house, that I think being polite is so easy, yet so important. Like I said in the Diary

Room, 'Please and thank you are only little words to say –
but they are big words to hear.'

This woman just grunted at me. I don't know why – I
don't think I did anything to merit it. Perhaps it was just
my age. But I kept thinking: 'If you had a young daughter,
would you want someone being so horrible to her?'

At one time I had a job in telesales, and they sacked me.
I cried my eyes out – which was funny because I was
planning to give my notice in on the day they told me to
leave. Dad picked me up from work that day, and I was in
floods of tears. He couldn't understand it.

'You should be happy – you wanted to leave,' he said.

'Yes, but I wanted to be the one who made the decision,'
I said. It wasn't that I was no good at telesales, but my heart
wasn't in it, and so my attitude was wrong. One important
factor was that the woman at the desk in front of me took
her shoes off on a really hot day. Her feet were stinking to
high heaven, and I was gagging.

'Oh, what's that smell?' I said, hoping she would take
the hint.

'Could be my feet,' she replied.

I felt like saying, 'If you know it's your feet, put some
shoes on, for God's sake!' But I didn't have the bottle to
say it.

Another time I worked at a call centre for a bank. It was
a happy place, and I got on with the other girls, but I gave
my notice in when I found a new job. The girls had all
nicknamed me Barbie, because by this time I was blonde,
so they stuck posters up everywhere saying 'Barbie's
leaving!' But I changed my mind about taking the new job,

and rang in and got my old job back. When I walked in again more posters went up: 'Barbie's back!' Everyone knew who it meant.

I did worry about changing my jobs so often. Many of my friends are in the same jobs they started when they left school, moving up through the companies they work for. I always seemed to be starting out again, always at the bottom of the ladder. But the jobs were never really right for me, and deep down I knew it. They were just a stopgap, something I had to do to earn some money before I started on my 'real' life. I still didn't know what that real life would be exactly, but I knew it didn't involve doing nine to five in an office.

When I was sixteen I decided I was going to redecorate my bedroom. I fancied the idea of doing it myself, and I convinced Mum to let me have a go – although I think she lived to regret the decision! I had a clear idea of how I wanted it to look, with a soft pink wash over white. It sounds lovely, doesn't it? Unfortunately, it didn't quite live up to the description. It looked terrible, a big mess. Still determined to do it myself, I painted it white again. Then I put some strong cerise pink at the top of the walls, and did the bottom half purple. It looked even worse. I'd managed to get the paint on to the coving at the top of the wall, and the colour didn't look the way I imagined it would. Mum's word for it was 'vile', and I'm forced to admit she was right. By this time there were so many coats of paint on the walls that they were beginning to peel off in lumps. It looked truly hideous, all scabby and disgusting. I'd completely ruined the room.

I'd even tried to put up shelves on my own. I was drilling into the wall between her bedroom and mine, which is only a plasterboard wall, and I remember having to go into her room to check that I hadn't drilled all the way through.

Mum is a good painter and decorator, but even she couldn't tackle the mess. She had to get a professional in to strip the walls of all the paint. Then she got her brushes out and painted it immaculately, in a lovely pink. It was what I'd wanted all along. Just recently, about a year ago, she was doing the house up.

'You don't want me to help, do you?' I said.

'No thank you,' she replied, very firmly, 'I'd rather you didn't.'

So much for my decorating skills.

I'm quite a tidy person, and even when I was a teenager I couldn't go to bed with my room a mess. I hate seeing loads of clothes all over the floor. But I am a bit lazy about hanging them up: my idea of tidying the room is to scoop them all up and put them in the dirty washing basket!

But if I was no good getting the right look in my bedroom, I was doing better with my own personal style – my hair, my clothes and my make-up. Although, I must admit, I wish I still had the thick, long hair that I used to have before I started having extensions put in.

My extensions are probably the most famous extensions in Britain, and it sometimes seems that every female journalist in the country has an opinion on them. Some of them love them, some of them are really rude about them. But they came about from necessity, not choice: I had every girl's worst nightmare, a hairdresser who took no notice of me and chopped my long hair off, when all I wanted was a trim to get rid of my split ends.

Like I've already said, my hair is naturally a dark brown colour, and it's always been long, from the time I was very small. I started having highlights put through it when I was sixteen, and before long I had so many that it was more or less completely blonde.

I was eighteen when I had the trim which turned out to be a major chop. I cried my eyes out. My hair had been really long, and now it hardly reached my shoulders. Everyone told me how good it looked, but I knew it didn't. The more they said it, the more I wanted to scream, 'It doesn't!' I know they were only trying to make me feel better, and that if I could have been patient it would have grown again. But my long hair is really important to me, it is part of how I see myself. Every time I looked in the mirror I saw a different person, and I didn't like it.

So that's when I started to have extensions. I was glad they existed. I went to a salon in Southend, Legends, and I became a regular, right up to after leaving the *Big Brother* house. I would still go back there, except that I don't live in the area any more.

I chose acrylic extensions because I like the look: they are thicker and blunter than the real hair extensions. A full head of extensions cost me £150, and I had them replaced every six weeks – another good reason why I needed to earn money. But to save spending six hours at the hairdresser at a time, I'd have some replaced after three weeks and the rest after another three weeks.

If you've never had them done, it's quite simple, but it does take time. The hairdresser takes a long strand of hair, glues the extension on and then melts it on to your real hair.

I do love my extensions, but they aren't good for your own hair, and eventually it becomes ratty and thin. I could cry when I think about the lovely thick, long hair I used to have.

Mum helped me out with the cost of the extensions, because even though I was working it was a great deal of money.

I started wearing make-up when I was about fourteen. Mum helped me choose the shades. I never had much money, but neither did my friends, so we'd buy lipsticks for £1.99 and then try out each other's colours. I really enjoyed messing about with make-up – and I still do. I'm really happy when I'm trying out new products.

I always wear bright lipstick, because it lifts things and makes me feel happy. I've experimented with more subdued shades, but they just don't have the same effect. If I was stranded on a desert island and only allowed one item of make-up, it would be lip gloss, definitely.

Nowadays, if I am in a hurry, it takes about fifteen minutes to do my make-up. I love appearing on television, because I like having my face made up by a professional. I ask them for advice, and I take note of the products they use if I think they work on me. The professional make-up artists can make me look so different, they can get looks that I can't recapture when I do it myself.

The thing that made the most difference was plucking my eyebrows when I was sixteen. I can't imagine why I didn't do it earlier. They are dark and naturally quite bushy, and I suppose I should have gone to a proper beautician to have them done. But I just picked up the tweezers and had a go myself, and the result was really good. It changed the whole shape of my face. Eyebrows are a great frame for the eyes, but if they are too dominant you don't really see the eyes. I instantly looked and felt better.

As far as clothes are concerned: if you've seen me on TV, you'll know what I like: bright, bright, bright. I'm always drawn to vibrant colours, and I love mixing them. I'll team an orange jacket with yellow trousers and a green top, and it looks great. I'd rather wear what suits me than follow a trend, although I keep up with all the latest fashion news.

But if something comes along that I don't like, I won't do it. I never got into the retro look, and I wouldn't have been seen dead in a pair of Ugg boots. I've got an instinct for what suits me. I always choose fairly fitted clothes, and I would hardly ever wear grey or any drab colour like that. If I wear black I always brighten it up with a splash of colour.

I've never been on a diet in my life, but I do eat fairly sensibly. I think diets are a bad idea. If I tried to go for a week without chocolate, I'd start obsessing about it, and I'd really be craving it. As it is, I don't pig out on chocolate and I may go for longer than a week without eating any, without worrying about it. If I fancy a piece of it, I'll have it.

I'm not the skinniest girl around, but I'm not fat. I haven't done any exercise until recently, but I've started now, mainly because I wanted to get myself toned for the wedding. I don't believe that you have to be skinny to be beautiful: curvy girls can look terrific. Everyone can make the most of their looks, and everyone can be beautiful in their own way.

A lot of beauty comes from within: if you feel confident about yourself, you look good. My mum always told me I was beautiful. She has always been there, reassuring me whenever I have had doubts about my looks.

I'm not a party girl, I don't enjoy getting wrecked in nightclubs. I feel I've been there, done that, and it didn't do anything for me. Nowadays, if I'm going out, I prefer to go for a meal or a quiet drink.

My dislike of nightclubs probably stems from a horrible, unprovoked attack on me when I was eighteen. To this day, I have no idea why I was targeted. Probably it was a case of mistaken identity – I can't think of any other explanation. But it was vicious and relentless, and it left me injured and in shock.

It happened at a nightclub in Basildon, a place my friend Lisa and I went most weekends. It was early, only about 9 p.m., and so the place was relatively empty. Most of the customers at that time were girls, although there were groups of blokes dotted about.

Lisa was talking to a girl I didn't know when I got there.

I'd never seen her before. I walked across to join them, expecting to be introduced and to have a friendly chat. But when I got near, the girl suddenly punched me in the face. It was so sudden and ferocious that I reeled backwards and fell to the floor, my shoes flying off. Then two other girls started kicking my legs as I scrambled to get up. The girl who had launched the attack was holding my head and kneeing me in the face and punching me.

The bouncers came over – they didn't seem to be in any hurry. One of them took hold of me, and, astonishingly, let the girl carry on punching me in the face while he held my arms. Then they dragged me away and literally threw me through some double doors into a small room, where I was told to cool off.

Nobody did anything to help me. When the attack was launched there were blokes standing around, and they just watched. After a few minutes the bouncers asked me what was going on, and I told them I hadn't a clue what had prompted the attack.

They escorted me out of the club, asking me to point out the girl who had attacked me. But I wouldn't in case it caused more trouble. The bouncers told me to leave – as if I would have wanted to stay! On my way out someone gave me my shoes.

I hadn't seen Lisa since the fight started, but she caught up with me outside. I was trembling with shock, my legs were like jelly, and my face felt as if I had been in the ring with Mike Tyson. I knew I had a black eye coming up, without looking at it. I could feel it swelling, and gradually closing.

We jumped into a cab and went back to Wickford. On the way home I rang for Mum, who quickly arrived and took me to hospital.

They X-rayed my skull, and told me that I had a fractured jaw. It wasn't a serious fracture, thank goodness. My legs were hurting, and you could already see the bruises coming up: by the following day I had a massive black eye, a swollen eyebrow, and legs that were black and blue.

But the shock was probably worse than the physical injuries. I was literally shaking when we got to the hospital. The staff there wanted to call the police, but I refused because I didn't want any more trouble.

I feel disgusted by the idea of girls fighting, and I feel ashamed to have been involved in a nightclub brawl with another girl. But I didn't start it, and to this day I don't know what it was all about. It could have been mistaken identity, or perhaps the girl just didn't like the way I looked. I'll never know the reason, and haven't seen the girl who attacked me since then.

It put me off going out. I don't think I went out again for at least six months. And when I do go to nightclubs, I'm always very uncomfortable, on edge, looking around to check who is behind me.

They say lightning doesn't strike twice, but I'm taking no chances. Besides, I've really grown out of the whole nightclub scene. Now, if I'm not busy working, there's nothing I enjoy more than a quiet night in.

Two good friends at this time were Louise and Emma, who had both been at school with me. Funny to think that when we were at school Louise scared me: we used to walk past each other in the corridors and try to stare each other out. But I met Emma again in a pub and we all became good friends. Emma and me went on holiday to Greece together – my first girlie holiday. I love sunbathing so much that one morning I went down to the hotel pool before it was even open. We didn't go clubbing, as neither of us was really into that, but we went to some bars in the evening. It was just great fun.

Nicole is another old school friend I still see. We used to go out, spend all our money and then have to walk miles to get home. Nicole is really funny, and is always making me laugh with stories of things that have happened to her.

Chapter Four

The Dream Unfolds

People would often tell me that I ought to be a model. In the jobs I had they would say: 'You shouldn't be here, you should be modelling.' I thought maybe they were right, and I knew that if I didn't give it a try while I was young it would be too late, and I might always regret it. But I had no idea how to go about becoming a model. I knew there were lots of risks: that if you're not careful, you can get ripped off, like we did with the child modelling 'agency', or find yourself working for sleazy people. I'd looked modelling up on the Internet, but there were so many agencies, and as an outsider you just don't know who to trust.

And there were personal reasons why my confidence was low at this time. I was in a relationship with a boyfriend who put me down, made me feel worthless, bullied me in a subtle (and sometimes not-so-subtle) way. What is it with me and bullies? But, like the girls at school, he ultimately strengthened me, and made me the person I am today. I'm actually grateful to him: he gave me my determination to succeed. And he also, by showing me what a bad relationship is like, taught me to never settle for second best in my personal life.

But enough of him: I'll deal with him later. What happened next in my working life is that I had a job as a receptionist at a company in Rochford, near Southend. It was a happy atmosphere, and once again quite a few people who met me there told me I ought to be modelling. One guy who was working there as an engineer, Gordon, was really into motorbikes. He was a dedicated biker, and he and his girlfriend used to go out on his bike every weekend. One day, he came in with a copy of *Motor Cycle News* which he thrust in front of me, on the reception desk.

'There you are, Chantelle,' he said. 'There's your big chance.'

The magazine was running a competition to find a group of girls to be their *Motor Cycle News* girls, and there was an entry form, which I cut out. I had to send off some photographs, so Mum took loads. I posed in a bikini, in a little skirt and top; we even took some action shots of me jumping up in the air in the garden. We took them at seven in the morning, as we both had to go to work, and I needed to get the film in to be developed that day.

It was six weeks before I heard anything, and I might have been giving up hope – except that I always had a good feeling about it. I was thrilled when I got a letter in December 2002, saying I'd been selected to go to the semi-finals in January. I was really excited, and had a very happy Christmas. I was careful with what I ate, because I wanted my skin to be at its best, and I gave myself lots of home beauty treatments, like face packs and hair masks.

The event was held at Alexandra Palace, in north London, and we were auditioned in public in the middle of a massive motorcycle show. Mum and my boyfriend came with me, and they were able to watch me from the audience. There were loads of girls there – I think there were twenty-seven of us altogether. We were given short skirts and Lycra tops to wear, in red, white and black, and with the logo for *Motor Cycle News*, a large MCN, on the front. Then we went onstage in turn, and were given a little interview by two guys. The questions were simple: what's your name? Where are you from? Why do you want to be in the *MCN* squad?

I said something like: 'It's the next step to getting where I want to be.' Which is exactly what it turned out to be. Then we had to sit astride a bike to have our pictures taken.

I loved it. I was a little bit tense, because I was so keen to get through, but I felt completely comfortable posing for pictures. I've never had a modelling lesson in my life, but it came naturally. At the end of the day I was thrilled to be told I was through to the finals. I rushed off to tell Mum, who said she knew all along I'd get through.

The finals were a week later, at the same place. We did everything exactly the same as we had done the week before: I stopped at the same shop for a bagel and a cup of tea, I wore the same clothes. I was desperate not to break my luck.

This time they had all the girls onstage together, eighteen of us. We each had a number, and we stepped forward in turn to introduce ourselves. Then we stood backstage while they called out the winners.

My number was 17, and the first one they called was 18. I thought, 'If they don't call mine now, that's it.' It was a very tense moment, but they didn't build up the suspense by pausing: my number was announced straight away. I was so relieved, I couldn't believe it. I walked back onstage with a huge smile on my face.

Ten of us were selected, and we were the *MCN* girls. We had been told at the very beginning that we would be appearing at a series of events, with a year's contract. I had to give up my other job, as I needed to be free to travel around the country. But one of the first people I rang when I got the news was Gordon. He was delighted that I had got through, and that they had been part of it. I have a great deal to thank Gordon for: he is the one that helped me on the first step towards living the dream.

It was more like promotions work than modelling, which was a bit disappointing, but I was completely happy to have achieved it. In my own way, I felt I had got somewhere. Through winning I was automatically on the books of a promotions agency, and they liaised with us about the events we had to attend. I think I went to about fifteen in the whole year, the furthest away being Edinburgh. We were paid £100 per event, plus expenses, so it was hardly the big time, money-wise. But it opened doors.

I got to know the other girls, and they were a nice bunch, we had a good laugh. It was great to be with people of my own age again, and people who shared my interest in make-up and hair and all those girlie things. I was specially friendly with a girl called Tanya. On the very first day she thought I was giving her dirty looks, and I thought she was giving me dirty looks. When we got to know each other we had a good laugh about it. I've lost track of Tanya – I think she must have lost her phone or changed her number, but we were good friends at the time.

Several of the girls were already established as models, and through them I was given the names of some reputable modelling agencies. I signed up to one, and they arranged for a professional photographer to take some pictures of me. I was beginning to build up a portfolio, which is what every model needs. I had the *MCN* photos, plus these, and some taken by my local paper, who wrote about me when I landed the *MCN* contract. The day they came to take pictures of me it was raining, so they took me to the local park and photographed me in wellies and with an umbrella. I couldn't stop laughing: there were nine-year-old boys wolf-whistling at me.

I tried some other agencies, as well. It was a dispiriting process. The people interviewing would look me up and down, look at my portfolio, ask me a few questions, but they mainly seemed indifferent, and when they turned me down some of them wouldn't even bother to explain why. If they did explain, it didn't always make sense.

I remember one agent saying, 'You're not the look we are looking for.' Then, in the next sentence, he said

'You're too like too many girls who are already on our books.'

That was a complete contradiction, yet he didn't even notice. I know now that lots of girls have to do the rounds before they find an agency, but at the time each rejection was really hurtful. I never thought they gave me just that little bit of a chance that I needed.

One of my ambitions was to be a Page Three girl. I know some people turn their noses up at topless modelling, but there is nothing sleazy about Page Three work. The photographers are very professional, the girls are always beautiful, and the topless bit is nothing more than you can see on any beach on holiday. I'd sunbathed topless many times, so why not get paid for it? I believe that what makes a picture tacky or sleazy is to do with the pose. If you do topless work for a big national newspaper, you are never going to be asked to do any pose that borders on soft porn. In modelling terms, I think it's a very prestigious thing to do.

Luckily for me, both Mum and Dad felt the same about it. When I started modelling professionally, they were concerned that I should be with a reputable agency, but they always trusted me. Mum knew I would never be persuaded into doing anything I wasn't comfortable with. I've always been strong like that: I'd never get talked into anything that wasn't right. If she really hadn't wanted me to do topless, I would have turned it down. But she, like me, felt it was an achievement to be asked to do it. And Dad always said he knew I would only do tasteful things, and that he trusted my judgement.

Once, I read about a competition for a Page Three girl, and you had to send in some pictures. So we went off to a park in Wickford one quiet afternoon, and Mum did some topless pictures of me. It was winter and getting quite dark, and as we left the park with armfuls of clothes we saw a police car parked nearby. We drove off, but they came after us and flashed the blue light for us to pull over. The two policemen wanted to know what we had been doing. We fell about laughing and explained. They had a good laugh, too, and said they would look out for me on Page Three.

The other girls I met at the *MCN* jobs gave me the names of some Page Three photographers, and I rang them all. I know they must get so many girls ringing up, but I was disappointed that the *Sun* photographer never rang me back. But the good news was that Jeannie Savage, the Starbird photographer for the *Daily Star*, got in touch and asked me to bring my book (my portfolio) in to show her.

My book was rubbish compared with most girls'. None of the pictures had been airbrushed (that's what photographers do to take out any blemishes) and, apart from the ones my agency organised, they weren't studio shots. But I could never afford to have really good pictures done. It was a catch-22 situation: because of my commitments to MCN I couldn't do a normal job, and so therefore I had very little money; and because I had very little money I couldn't afford to get decent pictures done for my book, which I needed to get more modelling work.

I took it along to the studio in Old Street, and thankfully Jeannie Savage could see my potential, and she invited me back to do test shots. I loved it. I just took to it straight

they wouldn't let their daughter do it, but Mum was cool. She just puts that sort of comment down to sour grapes.

We went to the local pub that night, and everyone was making a fuss. The *Star* didn't use my real name: they called me Paris, because I look like Paris Hilton. That's how I later had the idea of working as a Paris Hilton lookalike.

Dad was by this time running a veterans' football team, with all the players over thirty-five. When he went into the dressing room on Sunday to see his team, they had bought lots of copies of the *Star* and plastered my picture everywhere. Dad took it in good part: he knew the blokes were just having a laugh, and he didn't mind.

Jeannie Savage invited me back for another session, this time on my own. Each time, I couldn't wear a bra on the way to the studio: if you get the marks of bra straps it can take a while before they disappear. For a few weeks after the shoot I bought the *Daily Star* every day, and every day there was a feeling of disappointment when some other girl beamed out of the Starbird slot. My picture was never used.

You can't imagine how low I felt. It was crushing. I felt I had got so near. The world had landed at my feet, then it had been snatched away again. My *Motor Cycle News* contract also ended, so I was desperate for work. I was only paid £150 for the *Daily Star* sessions, and by the time the agency took their cut, there wasn't a lot to live on.

I did have one lovely job. A photographer called Jens Wikholm took eight girls to Majorca for a week. It was in May, and not very hot, but we had to look as though we were being pictured in the sunshine. It was fun, but I don't think I ever saw the pictures used – until I was in the *Big Brother* house, of course. I remember Jens saying to us all at the end of the week:

'Now all you have to do, girls, is get famous.' He knew that if any of us did, he would have a valuable set of pictures. Well, I didn't disappoint him!

I scraped along between modelling and promotions jobs, living from one £20 to the next. After I won *Celebrity Big Brother*, lots of people seemed to think that everything had just landed in my lap, that I became a celebrity without doing anything to deserve it. But the truth is I spent five years just getting by, struggling to survive.

I danced on a So Solid Crew video, and I did a photo session for a boy racers' magazine called *Max Power*, in which me and some other girls had to dance around speed cameras. (When I was in the house, these pictures were used in a newspaper under the headline 'FROM NICE GIRL TO VICE GIRL'. They tried to suggest that the shoot was me pretending to be a hooker – it was absolute rubbish.)

One day I found myself standing outside Waitrose in Southend promoting coffee machines, that was a low point. I felt I had lost my grip of the whole modelling thing. I'd almost made it, but I'd never really been given a chance.

I had run up some debts, mainly because you always have to look your best when you turn up for a job, and so I needed to keep my hair looking good, and have the right clothes and make-up. The bank was writing to me, because I was overdrawn. I'd also got bills for my mobile phone. It came to about £600 altogether, which is a lot when you have no money. Mum was very understanding, and tried to help out as much as she could. She knew I didn't want to go back into an office. She knew I dreamed of being someone, and she wanted it for me almost as much as I wanted it for myself. She always had faith in me, but I felt guilty being so dependent on her.

Being so broke all the time was really difficult. I never had much money for Christmas and birthday presents, I couldn't afford to go out, and if I went shopping with friends I had to watch while they bought all the latest trends. I took on part-time temporary jobs, like doing three lunchtimes a week behind the bar at a pub near home, the Duke. My dad's football team meet at the pub, and Dad knew they needed extra staff. But I never felt cut out to be a barmaid: you have to be very chatty and flirty all the time with complete strangers.

I got a little bit of work as soon as Paris Hilton started appearing more and more in the gossip columns and the celebrity magazines. When she came on the scene, all my friends, and even people I didn't know, told me how much I looked like her. Later on, when I was all over the newspapers, some journalist came up with the joke of calling me Paris Travelodge, meaning a cheaper, more downmarket version of Paris Hilton. They said it was a nickname used by my friends, but I never heard it before I read it in the papers, so I'm sure it's down to the wit of some reporter or other. I don't mind the name: it's just funny.

And of course the *Daily Star* had called me Paris when I was a Starbird. I began to get tired of hearing it, so in the end I phoned a lookalike agency, and sent them some pictures. I felt a bit embarrassed by it, but I thought nobody would know I was doing this kind of work, which didn't feel like real modelling to me. The only person I told was Mum.

The agency rang me immediately, asking to see the copyright of the pictures: they didn't believe I really looked so like her, and they suspected I'd cheated and sent in pictures of her. The first job I did was to walk around a toy exhibition carrying a cuddly dog: Paris famously walks around with her little dog.

Another job I landed was a promotion in Windsor on the day of Prince Charles's wedding to Camilla Parker Bowles. I never made it to their big day, because the evening before I walked out of a bar with a friend, and while crossing the road to get a taxi I ricked my ankle. I know what you're thinking – but I was NOT drunk. I'd gone there to meet my friend, Rachael, and she'd had a few drinks. When she got me to hospital, with a horribly swollen ankle, I was given a wheelchair, and she was barging her way through doors using my legs to open them! I was shrieking in pain, but laughing at the same time because it was like something out of a comedy film. Luckily, there wasn't anything seriously wrong with my ankle, but it was swollen up like a balloon and I was told I had to rest it for a few days, which meant I had to miss the job in Windsor. I've no idea what I was supposed to be doing there, apart from pretending to be Paris Hilton. Perhaps it's as well I didn't go, because I've met Prince Charles since.

The sad bit about being at the hospital was seeing three

old ladies, on trolleys in the corridor. They didn't have any friends or family with them. One kept asking where she was, so Rachael rubbed her hand and said, 'It's all right, you'll be OK.' It was heartbreaking leaving them there. I'm full of admiration for nurses and people who work in caring professions. I suppose you get used to it, but it would break my heart every day to see such suffering.

The Paris Hilton work was a low point for me. It wasn't what I wanted to be doing, and, on top of that, it caused me some real problems with my hair. At that time, and all through my earlier modelling days, I had my hair blonde on top but I kept it dark, with a mixture of blonde and dark extensions, underneath. When I went for the agency photoshoot, the woman in charge wanted me to be blonde all over, so I had to take out the dark extensions and a hairdresser, who was at the shoot, sprayed the rest of it to make it blonde.

Except that it didn't go blonde: it went orange. I told him there was a dark tint on it, but he carried on doing it. My hair was ruined – and as you have probably worked out by now, if there is anything wrong with my hair, I am really upset. I was in tears, but he told me he was a top hairdresser, and that he would take me back to his salon and neutralise the colour. He was telling me that it looked lovely, but it certainly didn't. I was distraught.

When we got to the salon he started to put neutraliser on, but it was late in the evening and there was no one else there. My hair was ruined, and all I wanted to do was go home. So I walked out, and made my way to the nearest tube station with tears running down my face.

The next day my hairdresser sorted it out, giving me blonde extensions all over.

I have only been in love once in my life – real, deep, heart-churning love. And there are no prizes for guessing who that is with.

But, obviously, I was twenty-two by the time I went on *Celebrity Big Brother* and met Preston, so I had been out with other boys before then. I'd have to have been a nun to not have! I'd had one serious relationship, which lasted for more than three years, and ended almost a year before I went into the house.

It was not a happy relationship. I knew from the very beginning that I should never have been in it, and every single day I thought about how it was wrong. I suppose at the beginning I thought I was in love, but it soon became a destructive relationship.

He put me down all the time, in lots of ways. He destroyed my confidence, made me feel that my dreams were silly. I used to fantasise about the day I could turn to him and say:

'Yeah, look at me now, I've proved I am somebody, I *can* do something with my life.'

But, do you know what? Now that day has come I really don't care what he thinks. I wouldn't be thinking about him now, except that it would not be honest to write this book and pretend the relationship never happened. I'm not even going to put his name in here – I wouldn't give him the satisfaction of a namecheck. When I force myself to look back at that time, I realise just how wrong he was for me, and how damaging the relationship was to my self-esteem. He made me feel he was doing me a favour being with me, and I was so young and naive I just went along with it.

The only thing he gave me was an absolute determination to succeed. He made me strong, in the same way that the bullies in school made me strong. It was, in fact, a bullying relationship, one in which he tried to control me.

I met him in a pub, a week before my eighteenth birthday. I was with some mates and he was with some mates, the usual sort of thing. He was a few years older than me. Looking back, I can't think what I even saw in him, but obviously at the beginning I must have felt attracted to him.

He was really pleased when I landed the *MCN* job, and supportive when my picture was in newspapers or magazines, but when things weren't going so well for me he never encouraged me, simply said I should get a proper job, earn some money. But it was not his decision what I did, and his attitude made me even more determined to persevere with my dream.

He cheated on me time and time again, and treated me like dirt and acted as if he didn't care if it upset me. He probably didn't realise how unhappy I was: it just became the way our relationship was. From the very beginning he seemed to have a hold over me, making me feel I needed him. But at the same time, every single day of the time I was with him, I knew it was wrong.

He made me feel I wasn't pretty, or attractive. I used to

go to modelling jobs trying to look confident, but inside me there was this little voice reminding me that I couldn't possibly be good enough. I had to tell myself I shouldn't be feeling like this.

I want to be honest about this, because I believe there are lots of girls (and even married women) trapped in relationships with men who work at eroding their self-confidence, taking away all their personality and all the things that they dream about. These men are poisonous, but when you are in the grip of the relationship they make you feel you can't leave. It's psychological bullying.

I was weak letting the relationship go as long as it did, but I felt I needed him. That's the subtlest kind of bullying of the lot: people like this make you lose sight of your own strengths. When we had a row, he had a great knack of turning it round so that I was always to blame, even though he was the one who had cheated or whatever.

Towards the end of the relationship we started living together. He rented a flat that belonged to a friend of his. It should have been a magical time, being together properly. For me it was my first experience of living away from home. But the good days were far outweighed by the bad days, and it was definitely the worst year of my life. The stupidest thing I ever did was splitting up with him and then being talked into going back.

It ended when I finally had the courage to leave for good. It was hard: he'd so destroyed my confidence that I felt nobody else would want me. Perhaps that sounds difficult to believe. But that's what bullying is all about: it's about destroying what's on the inside, not the outside.

Looking back, if I'd been in a supportive relationship, my modelling career might have blossomed. I know that half the battle in terms of looking good is how you feel about yourself. If you feel you look great and are great, that will come through in the way you make an impression on others.

But I have no regrets about the relationship. You have to experience unhappiness to truly appreciate happiness. You also need a spur to drive your ambitions, and, like the bullies at school, he gave me that spur. Through all the bullying experiences, I developed an inner strength. I may look fragile and like a dizzy blonde, but inside I am a strong person who now has a great sense of my own worth.

That's what everybody should have. If I can offer any advice to young girls it is: believe in yourself, and never let anyone destroy those beliefs.

The relationship ended when I finally packed my things and walked back to Mum's house. I'd found out he had been cheating on me again, and I said: 'That's it, I'm off now.'

He didn't seem to care. He just said: 'There are loads of other girls out there.'

I walked out of the door and he stood outside, waving me goodbye with a sarcastic grin on his face.

'Bye, see you later, have a good walk home,' he said.

I didn't have a lot of stuff to carry – I'd always kept most of my things at home, which shows I was never that committed to being with my boyfriend. I left things behind, but I wasn't worried: all I wanted was to get away.

As I walked home I was thinking, 'That is it. I'm free. You can't do this to me any more. I don't need you.'

I can remember walking in to Mum's kitchen and I started to cry, really sobbing. I leaned against the kitchen units and just slid down and sat on the floor, sobbing my heart out. It was such a relief to be home, and I felt as if a great weight had been lifted off me.

Mum and my stepdad Dean (I'll tell you about him in a minute) didn't know what to say, how to comfort me. Mum sat on the floor with me, holding me. I had reached the depths, but from there I could only go up.

I slept well that night, and the next morning, when I woke up, I felt really free. I never missed him or regretted leaving him: it was a wonderful release.

Mum had always known he wasn't the right person for me, but she is wise enough to know that I had to find that out for myself. Looking back, she has told me that while I was with him I lost some of my natural sparkle, and it was really hurting her to see me being brought down. She was very upset to see me so distraught when I moved back home, but for my sake she was also relieved that I was putting him behind me.

Those first weeks back at home were the worst of my life. Not because the relationship had ended – that was a real relief – but because I felt my dreams were fading fast and my career still wasn't on track. I could see everything I'd wanted slipping away from me, and I thought more and more about ending it all. I felt tired. I was constantly on the phone, ringing what I now know are stupid adverts saying

'Models Wanted'. I was continuously hounding model agencies asking if there were any castings happening, and when they said no I was sure that there were, and I was simply not being put forward.

I literally didn't know what to do. For a while it felt like I was in a daze. I just needed a chance – why wouldn't anyone give me one? I would sit at home on my own while everyone else was at work, and I felt like a failure. I had been living on hope and prayers, and nothing had come of it. It was the worst I had ever felt, and I was honestly beginning to feel I didn't have the strength to carry on. Who do you ring when you've called every model agency there is and they don't want to take you on?

I knew I'd never do it, but I did have thoughts about not being here any more, escaping from it all. Everyone knew what I wanted, and I felt stupid for not having achieved it. Every morning I'd wake up and think, 'Who can I ring? What can I do?' Many times I thought about the ultimate answer: I didn't think about how to do it, but I knew why I wanted to do it. But I also knew why I couldn't: because of my family. And also, despite everything, there was still something inside me that wouldn't give up. There were too many people who had affected my life, and given me this burning desire to prove myself and prove them wrong.

Mum knew how I felt, and I cried in her arms many times. She understood my feelings, and she would cry, too. What do you say to your daughter when she tells you that she doesn't want to live any more? She would ring me from work sometimes, and I knew there was no real reason: she was just checking that I was OK.

I know that you get cards which say 'The Best Mum in the World' – well, I couldn't say a truer word about my mum. She was there for me throughout my toughest times, and I'm so glad she was. I don't know how I would have coped without her.

Over the next few months I went out on a few dates, but there was nobody special. While I was on *Celebrity Big Brother* lots of men sold stories to newspapers about how they had been my boyfriend. I didn't get upset about it – it's just funny, isn't it? Can you imagine reading stories about how wild you are in bed, written by some guy you have never even met? Good luck to them, for duping newspapers into paying them money for that rubbish.

I was doing a personal appearance at a nightclub in Southend, soon after I came out of the house, and I ended my little speech on stage by saying:

'By the way, if any of the men who sold stories about how they've slept with me are in tonight, please make yourselves known to me. It would be nice to meet you!'

When I first appeared in the *Celebrity* house, and my face was all over the newspapers, my ex rang Mum and begged her to keep his name out of it. As if Mum would be telling the world about him! But, guess what? A week or two later, he sold his story about our relationship to the *News of the World*. So much for not wanting to be involved. The story was all about our sex life – and it was all untrue. He even said I rang him the night before I went into the house – as if. My last contact with him (my only contact after I left him) was about a month before, when I realised that I had left some shoes that I wanted at the flat. But I don't care about him saying what he did: I hope he enjoyed spending the money it made him. I just laughed when I read it.

It's amazing how people want a piece of someone else's fame. Even the boy I went out with when I was at school tried to sell his story. He went round to Mum's house and spoke to her, and she got the impression that he was trying to ask her for something, but she didn't know what. Half an hour after he left, his mother turned up on the doorstep and asked Mum if she could have a picture of the two of us together. She said her son would get £3,000 from a newspaper if he had a picture to prove he was my boyfriend. What a cheek! Mum certainly wasn't handing out pictures.

He never did sell his story, so he never got his £3,000. But some of the others, who did manage to sell their stories, didn't have pictures of themselves with me – largely because it would have been impossible, as I didn't even know who they were!!!

My relationships may not have been working out, but I'm happy to report that Mum was having better luck. She'd been single for about five years, and had coped brilliantly looking after me and Gregg on her own. But she deserved to be happy, and so I was delighted when she told me she had met a new man.

I would have welcomed Dean into our family just because he made my mum happy. But when I got to know him I really, really liked him. What's not to like? He's a great guy, and just right for Mum.

They met on a Sunday night. Mum wasn't very keen on going out, but a friend persuaded her to pop out for a drink. Dean, who works for a removal company, was flying off on holiday to Tenerife the next day, and so he had planned to stay home and get on with his packing. So it was a miracle they met, because neither of them really intended to be there.

It was about three weeks after they got together that Mum introduced him to me and Gregg. We both took to him, and when he moved in it felt like the best possible thing in the world. He and Mum aren't actually married, but I think of Dean as my stepdad. He'll never replace my dad, and he wouldn't want to. But he's very special.

I wish Dad could also find someone to settle down with. He's had girlfriends since he and Mum split, but nothing serious. He's a great guy, and I'm sure one day he'll settle down with the right lady. Because Dad's flat is not far from Mum's house in Wickford, I used to pop round two or three times a week to see him – but I must admit it has been not quite so often since I came out of the *BB* house. That's only because I have been so busy, and I'm not spending much time in Wickford. But we talk all the time on the phone.

Dad was very supportive of me during the years when I was struggling to get somewhere. Whenever I went for a modelling job, I'd ring him up and ask him how to get there. Being a taxi driver, he has an encyclopedic knowledge of London, so if ever I'm lost I ring him and he tells me which direction to walk to the nearest tube station. It's one of the risks of his job – it's not just me who rings him for help, but all his friends and relatives.

It was Dean who first told me to 'Live the dream'. He always said it, when I was going out to a modelling job, or just out for a drink with friends. He'd say it to Mum, too, but after a while it became something he mostly said to me. Then Mum would say it, too.

'You know what Dean says, go and live the dream.'

So I did . . .

Chapter Five

Big Brother: Please Let Me In

The audition for *Big Brother 6* was on Mother's Day, March 2005. If my mum had been around, I would probably just have stayed home to be with her. But luckily (as it turned out) she was going out for the day, so I was at home on my own.

I'd read about the auditions, which are staged all over the country. The one nearest to me was at the Excel exhibition centre, in London's Docklands. The *Big Brother* team auditioned there on the Saturday and the Sunday, and the auditions closed at 3 p.m. on the Sunday. I arrived at twenty to three. It really was a last-minute thing, and it was a last-minute decision by me to go.

I was at a low ebb. It was just before the horrible break-up with my boyfriend, my modelling career didn't seem to be going anywhere, and I'd been forced to take a normal job in telesales for an insurance company just to keep myself afloat, and to try to build up some savings so that I could get a good portfolio of pictures together. I'd been thinking everything over quite seriously, and I'd decided to give myself one more year to break into the sort of career I really wanted.

If, at the end of that year, I'd failed, then I told myself I would stick with a regular job and accept that I would never fulfil my dream. At least I would know I had tried.

So it was in this spirit that I set off on my own for the audition. I'd watched *Big Brother 5* all the way through, and I'd loved every minute of it. I'd also watched some of the earlier series, but I'd never become hooked on them like I had the previous summer. Best of all, I'd really loved the *Celebrity Big Brother*, with Caprice, Kenzie and the others, and it was definitely this one that inspired me to apply. (I always thought the celebrity version was better than the ordinary one, but I never dreamed that one day I'd end up in the house with a bunch of famous people.)

Anyway, I told myself, the audition would be interesting. I rang Dad and asked him how to find the place, and I rang Mum to tell her I was setting off. I didn't agonise over what to wear: I just put on a pair of jeans, a peach-coloured top and a grey denim jacket. I was so broke I had to go through my pockets and rummage at the bottom of my bag for spare coins to pay the train fare.

There was a queue of about 150 people when I got there, and eventually we were called out in groups of eight. First we faced questions from a couple of members of the production team – random questions about our lives, things we had done, what we wanted to do. Then we were asked to line up and one lad was told to rank us according to how ugly we were. I'd have hated having to do that, but he entered into the spirit of it. Then we were put in pairs and had to ask each other questions.

I was asked several times why I wanted to be on *Big Brother*, and the only answer I could give was the honest one: 'I don't know.' I genuinely didn't know.

One of the production staff who was supervising my group was Sharon Powers, the Executive Producer, although I had no idea about this at the time. She told me and one other guy from my group that we were through to the next round: the others all had to go home. I didn't have a clue about the audition process, and to me getting through one round meant that I was practically in the *Big Brother* house. I texted Mum, really excited. From what I know now, I realise I was still miles away.

We had to fill in a big form, giving masses of details about ourselves, then we went into a mock-up of the Diary Room, to say to camera what sort of people we were and why we wanted to be on *Big Brother*. We had to talk for thirty seconds. I simply said my name and, again, that I didn't know why I wanted to be on the show. I think I actually left some of the tape blank, so I was convinced I had blown it. I could hear other people from my group recording their tapes, and they were all saying things like, 'I'm mad, me, I'm the maddest person you've ever met.'

As soon as the last of my group of ten had finished in the Diary Room, a few from the group were told they were through to the next stage, and the rest of us went into a big room. There were loads of people in there, and from time to time someone would call out some more numbers of lucky people who went to join the successful ones. My number wasn't called. I was gutted, and I trudged back to the tube station feeling very low. Another dream had been shattered. I tried ringing Mum, but she didn't pick up. I had to travel home on a packed train, standing most of the way, and feeling absolutely miserable.

It was eight o'clock that evening, when I was back at home, that my mobile rang. A man's voice came on, and told me that he was from *Big Brother* and that they would like to call me back for another audition the following Thursday. I thought it was a wind-up, one of my friends having a laugh. But I hadn't told anyone apart from Mum, Dad and Dean that I was going, and the man on the phone assured me it was real, so in the end I had to believe him.

The next audition was at Excel again. This time I really worried about what to wear. I chose a basque that was very tight, so tight I could hardly breathe, but I knew it looked good. It was floral-patterned, in cream and blue and brown, and I teamed it with the same jeans and jacket that I wore the first time.

When I arrived at 11 a.m. I was given a number and taken through to be interviewed, first on my own and then in a group of eight. Everyone had to say what they thought about the others, and they would pull different people out and put others in, to change the mix. I was pulled out at one time, and I had to go for a chat with another of the production team. Science, who later went into *BB6*, was at this audition.

'Stop arguing about everything,' I wanted to tell him. But

later, when I watched him in the house, I thought he was brilliant, a genius choice. He was one of my favourites of *BB6*.

At one point they said we could relax as my group wouldn't be needed again for two hours, so I went to the toilet and took the basque off. Just as I fastened the jacket up, they suddenly called my name again, and I had to quickly struggle back into it, with one of the researchers telling me to hurry up.

I went home that day feeling really excited. All they had told us was that they would let us know. I kept telling myself I may never hear from them, but I was hoping that I would. Luckily, they didn't keep me in suspense for too long: the phone rang two days later, and I was invited to the third round of the auditions. This time it was at an office in Tottenham Court Road.

I wanted to buy a new basque: I'd seen one in an ivory colour that I really liked. I had a temporary office job, and the day before I went for the audition Mum drove over in her lunchtime, picked me up from the office and drove like mad to the market where I'd seen the basque. I tore through to the stall, bought it, jumped in the car and made it back to work. Neither of us even had time to buy a sandwich!

There were thirteen of us there for the third round and we were first put into groups to play games. We had to build a tower out of newspapers, to see which group could get it the highest. Then we had to write two things about everyone else in the group, one positive thing and one negative thing. We also had to write why we thought it, and then stick it on their back, so they wouldn't know who said what.

When I read mine the negative comments were not too bad: one said I was 'a bit orange', which was a reference to my fake tan. Another said I looked like 'a blonde bimbo'. I didn't mind at all – it was really hard coming up with things to write.

I know they change the format of the auditions every time, and they use different games, so I don't think I'm giving away any trade secrets by describing what it was like.

Afterwards I met Sharon Powers again, and Phil Edgar-Jones, the Creative Director for all programmes made by Endemol, the company which makes *Big Brother*. Phil asked me how I would cope if I went into the house.

'I'd just go in with my eyes wide open,' I said.

'You'd better, or you'll bump into things,' he said.

It was very relaxed and light-hearted. I wasn't nervous: I didn't want to be annoyed with myself later for messing it up because of nerves. They filmed the interview (bits of it were later used as my introduction 'speech' when I went into *Celebrity Big Brother*).

Then I had to have a session with a psychiatrist: everybody who goes into the *Big Brother* house has to be screened to make sure they will be able to survive mentally in there. It was all a bit secretive, as at this stage the *Big Brother* staff were worried about the press tracking down the new housemates. I was told to go to the Embankment and sit on a certain bench, and someone would meet me. It was like being in a spy film. I was flicking through a magazine looking at pictures of all the glamorous girls, wishing it was me.

'Maybe one day,' I thought.

Then a researcher came and took me to the hotel, where the psychiatrist was meeting the would-be contestants. The session was weird for me, because I've never done anything like that. You sit in a room with a complete stranger who asks you all sorts of very personal questions. He asked me what sort of person I am, and then gave me examples of situations and asked how I would cope with them. He asked how close I was to my parents and my brother, and wanted to know all about my school life. It was quite probing, but I wasn't at all uncomfortable.

I went home without knowing whether I was in or not. I just had a big want inside me. I really, really wanted it.

About a week later I got a phone call from one of the production team, just checking to see that I was all right. It made me very hopeful that I had finally got somewhere, and I began to think seriously about the prospect of spending my summer in the *BB* house. They'd stressed to me how important it was that I didn't tell anyone, so I had to keep my excitement to myself – apart from Mum and Dean.

The time drew nearer and nearer for the start of the show, but I didn't worry: I knew they wouldn't tell the housemates until quite close to the date, to stop it leaking to the press. Eventually I was phoned again, and this time I was told that I would be going into the house a week before *Big Brother* began, as a 'guinea pig'. I didn't know what it meant. But it seems that, before the show starts, they always do a session with people living full-time in the house, in order to test all the cameras, the microphones, to check that the furniture is in the right place, and to give the massive number of people who work round the clock on *Big Brother* a practice run.

I was told about two weeks before I had to go in, so I quickly booked a holiday from work. The only people who knew what was going on were Mum and Dean, and they were almost as excited as I was. When I got the news I bought a cheap bottle of sparkling wine – I couldn't afford champagne – and we celebrated. I told Gregg I was going to Spain for a modelling shoot – but when I got back I had to hastily make up another story about going to see a friend, because I'd stupidly left my passport on the bedside table in my bedroom and he realised I hadn't gone abroad. I hate lying – which might seem funny to anyone who watched me act my way to being a celebrity. But I do. And I really had to dig myself into a hole, telling Gregg I'd made up the story about Spain to tell Mum. That's exactly why I hate lies – they tend to get bigger and more complicated the longer they go on, and I've never been any good at them.

I was so excited, going into the house, even as a guinea pig. A car came to collect me at 8 a.m., and took me to the studios at Elstree, which are right next door to the house. We were all kept in separate dressing rooms during the day. There was no TV or radio, but I had some magazines to leaf through. A researcher brought food and drinks, and chatted to me, but most of the time I was on my own, with my excitement mounting. We went through exactly the same procedure as if we were going in for real. My luggage was checked and itemised, my phone was taken away – but not before I sent one last text to Mum.

I took plenty of clothes, fake tan and other beauty products, even for a one-week stay. I didn't take any luxury items – as I don't smoke and don't drink a lot, I didn't really think about it. I should have taken wine for everyone to drink.

Twelve of us went in, all strangers to me – there weren't any from my round of the auditions. *Big Brother* chose me to perform a secret mission: I had to make people nominate me so that I'd get evicted. The only way I thought I could achieve this was to be horrible about the other housemates.

I found it hard, but decided to treat it as if I was acting a part. I really was a terrible housemate. I told one girl she had 'childbearing hips' and another that he looked 'like a pillar box in that jumper'. I was a real pain, not doing any jobs around the house, moaning about everything, all sorts of irritating things. I knew that to be in with a chance of being in the proper programme, I had to prove that I was willing to obey Big Brother, even if it made me unpopular.

Thankfully, I managed to persuade everyone in there to nominate me, and after three days I was evicted. Of course, I would have liked to stay a little bit longer, but I knew that by being evicted I'd proved my acting ability. I was genuinely pleased to hear my name being called:

'Chantelle, you have been evicted. Please leave the *Big Brother* house.'

When I first went into the house, what really struck me was how bright and whacky it was, just how I had imagined it. Everyone who has ever been on *Big Brother* comments on how quickly you forget that you are on camera the whole time, and it's true, especially in the living areas. In the toilet I was always acutely aware that someone was watching me, and once in the bedroom I saw a curtain twitch behind a mirror. But the rest of the time, even in my short, three-day stay, I forgot I was being filmed.

It was hard living in an environment where there was lots of screaming, shouting and giggling, especially when you were trying to sleep. There was nowhere to get away from the relentless fun they all seemed to be determined to have. I sometimes want to have a bit of a quiet time, not doing anything in particular. The other housemates all seemed to be on a high the whole time.

Even when I wanted to join in, I couldn't, because I had to seem miserable.

Looking back, I can see that the production team were trying me out for *Celebrity Big Brother*. I'd proved I could fool people, and they didn't need to see it any more. I had no idea at the time what it was all about, but somehow I knew I had done well.

It wasn't a proper eviction – there was no Davina moment. Afterwards, I had a chat with Sharon and some other members of the production team. They were all laughing at the way I had conned the others. They told me that I was a standby for the main series, and I signed a standby contract. Then a car took me home.

The next day I remember thinking: 'Yesterday I was in the *Big Brother* house, now I'm home and it's all over, but

I'm not allowed to tell anyone.' I was very disappointed to be a standby, but also fairly confident that I would still get to go in. I was sure someone would drop out.

I went back to work the following Monday, and I had to lie to my colleagues about my holiday.

'Did you have a good time?' they'd ask.

'Yes, it was really nice,' I'd say. More practice at acting for me – I was becoming accomplished at it! But I like to think it was not lying, it was acting.

I spent the whole summer watching *BB* avidly, with my fingers crossed that someone would walk out and I'd be able to go in.

Finally I got a call asking me if I would be available on the next Friday, which turned out to be the day when Orlaith, Kinga and Eugene went in. But when the Friday arrived no call came. It was so close to the end of the series that I knew it was my final chance. I felt very low. It seemed to be the story of my whole career, to get very near but never to quite make it. I always seemed to get a taster of what it would be like, only to have it pulled away from me. I was really down.

'That's that. I've had my chance,' I thought.

I was invited up to Elstree for the final night of *BB6*. I went on my own, but I knew some people there because there were others I had met in the guinea-pig house. Luckily, I told them I was playing a game when I was nasty to them, so they were all friendly. I didn't stay long. I simply wanted to show my face, but I was determined not to end up drinking too much and regretting it later.

I'd told my dad about it towards the end of the *Big*

Brother run, when it looked as though I might be going in, and after it was all over I told Gregg. But I didn't confide in any of my friends: they might not have believed me, and anyway, what was the point of telling everyone about my misfortune?

There was only one reason I was glad that I was at home, not in the house, that summer. Boycey, our beloved dog, died. He was sixteen and a half years old, and he'd been there, part of our family, for as long as I could remember. When you walked into our house he'd come to greet you, his little tail wagging like mad, and the first thing we said, all of us, was, 'All right, Boycey?'

Although he was old, he'd always been healthy. But Mum noticed that he was having fits, just little ones. We really hoped he would get better because we knew that if we took him to the vet, because of his age, he would probably have to be put to sleep. But when he didn't improve we had to make the decision. I believe it is cruel to keep an animal alive if it is suffering, but it was the hardest decision we've ever had to make. I went with Mum and Dean to take him to the vet, and I'll always remember saying goodbye, while he was laid out on the operating table. It was terrible. I cried for two weeks. I'd go out with friends and then I'd think about him and I'd have to go home. Walking into the house was horrible without Boycey there to greet me. Even now, I still half expect to see him when I go in.

(I'm too busy right now to have a dog. But I would like to, one day – except that, somehow, it would feel disloyal to Boycey. There can never be a dog to replace him.)

Another thing that happened to me during the *Big Brother* run was that I entered the Miss Greater London competition. I've never before or since entered a beauty contest, but I put myself forward after seeing it advertised on the website of a photographer I had worked with. A local car company sponsored me, because I knew someone who worked there. It was at the Café de Paris. I had to buy an evening dress to parade in, and I also had to wear a swimsuit that the organisers gave me. There were about twenty-five girls in it, but I didn't make it to the final three. I learned one thing from it: I don't ever want to be a beauty queen. It was a completely different world from modelling, and I didn't like it much. I didn't like lining up onstage and being compared to others. It was all very competitive.

I was not enjoying the telesales job, so I left and took a job working for a cosmetics company, Helen É, demonstrating make-up in Debenhams, in Oxford Street. My job was showing women how to apply cosmetics, which came naturally to me. I'd always been interested in make-up, and it was fascinating to see how I could transform people's faces. I mostly enjoyed the job because it was different – I definitely didn't want to go back to an office job. Again, I thought about training as a beautician, but the courses were all very expensive and I was struggling to pay off my debts – I certainly didn't want more.

The Helen É job was not full-time: I only went about three days a week, and I could choose when I would work. It was really another promotional job, and I was still

This photo was taken
by my friend Danielle.

At Bromford's High School,
aged fourteen.

Me, Emma and Nicole, all aged fourteen,
pretending to be the Spice Girls!

Me, aged seventeen, on holiday with my friend in Tenerife – nice lipstick!

My outfit to the leavers' ball in 1999.

Me and Nicole, out for a few drinks.

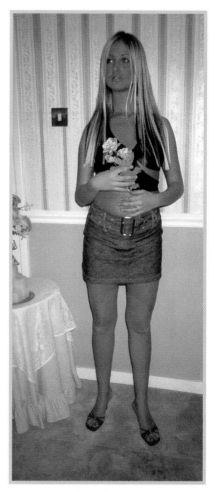

A photo my mum took to enter
me for the MCN competition.

Another modelling snap –
what was I thinking?!

With Mum and Dean,
at home in Essex.

At home on my
21st birthday.

In my outfit for the
Miss Great Britain
contest last year.

My big brother!

Me and my mum – two peas in a pod!

With Gregg in Brighton, March 2006 ... and when we were kids.

In a strategically pinned piece
of material!

Out in Essex with Rachael
for a work party in 2005.

A night out in London in 2005.

A night out in London with Rachael
in 2005. We travelled by limo.

The moment I had been waiting for – going into the *Big Brother* house.

Me, Preston and
Jodie chilling out.

Me with George
and Preston, who
is wearing Rula's
'Pants of Power'.

Me and Michael
Barrymore – off
the telly!

Kissing Preston
in the Diary
Room with Traci
– MMWAHH!

getting one or two of those. I'd put all my modelling and promotional work on hold because I wanted to keep myself free during the *Big Brother* run, in case I was called into the house, but now I was available for work again, and the most exciting thing I did was appear on Sky Sports' *Soccer AM* as a Soccerette. The Saturday morning programme regularly has girls on, dressed in the football strip of their favourite team. Naturally, mine was Arsenal – I think Dad and Gregg would never have spoken to me again if I'd worn any other strip! I had to take the shirt off, and underneath I was wearing a little white T-shirt with 'Easy' written on it in pink letters, which viewers could ring in and win.

Funnily enough, Preston has appeared on the programme several times, as they always have a band on. It would have been really weird if he had been on the show the day I was there: it would have completely blown me out when I was pretending to be a celebrity in the house. Thank goodness, on the day I appeared, the band was Hard-Fi. (I met them again recently and they all remembered me being on with them. Joe Swash, who plays Mickey Miller in *EastEnders*, was also on the programme, and I've met him since, too.)

I had given myself one year to make it, and the clock was ticking. It was beginning to look as though I would have to accept that my dream was never going to happen. Every time I went off to a modelling or promotions job, Mum and Dean would say 'Live the dream, Chantelle,' but it was starting to have a hollow ring to it. I just couldn't think how to move forward, and I really felt that the agencies simply hadn't give me a proper chance.

But then, in November 2005, I had a mysterious phone call. Mum was at work, and she called me to say that someone had rung her mobile, trying to get hold of me. That wasn't too unusual, as the phone Mum was using used to be mine, so she did get calls for me from time to time. Mum didn't know who it was, but it was a woman called Sam, and she wondered if it might be from an agency.

I was at home: it wasn't one of my days demonstrating make-up in Debenhams. I had a feeling as soon as I saw the number that it was something to do with *Big Brother*. I'd had so many secret phone calls in the summer, and I remembered meeting a researcher called Sam when I came out of the guinea-pig house.

I kept repeating to myself: 'Please, please let it be good news.' I so wanted something to happen, something to put my life on the track I wanted to be on. The phone call lit the flame of wanting inside me again. I tried to be cool, making myself wait a minute or two before ringing. But that was no good: I just had to make the call.

It was Sharon Powers, the Executive Producer, who answered. My chest started pounding, and I'm sure my voice went up a whole pitch in excitement. Sharon asked me how I was, and we chatted for a few minutes. I really didn't know what it was all about. She asked me what I had planned for January, and I told her there was nothing special, it would just be more of the same kind of work I was doing. She briefly said I should try to keep myself free for most of the month. There was nothing definite about it, and no explanation. Then she said she would call me again in three weeks, told me not to tell anyone about our conversation and that was it.

When I put the phone down, I couldn't make sense of it. I knew the only thing that happened in January, as far as *Big Brother* was concerned, was the celebrity edition. I wondered if the TV company, Endemol, were thinking of doing another reality show, but it didn't seem likely that they would do it at the same time as *Celebrity Big Brother*. I'd read stories in newspapers and magazines about the latest celebrity show, but I hadn't paid too much attention to the actual dates. So I typed '*Celebrity Big Brother*' into the Internet, and up it popped. Yes, the dates were identical with the ones Sharon had told me to keep free.

I couldn't believe it. I kept saying, over and over, 'Please let it be. Please.'

I started to be really hopeful again that something was going to happen, but I kept on reminding myself not to get too excited. Things had a habit of being whipped away from me at the last minute, so I was determined not to set myself up for too much of a fall. I tried to keep very cool, and just get on with my life for the next three weeks.

True to her word, Sharon rang me in the first week of December. She arranged to meet me two days later, at a hotel in Watford, on a Friday. I wore jeans and a bright green top. I got there by train, and a researcher met me and took me by taxi to the hotel. There were a couple of other *Big Brother* executives there.

They told me that it was about *Celebrity Big Brother* and

they hinted that they were thinking of putting half celebrities and half non-celebrities in. There was a camera there, and they filmed me, throwing different questions at me about how I would feel being in the house with celebrities, what sort of people I like, how I would react to famous people. (Bits of this interview were also used when I introduced myself before the show.)

Sharon said she would call me on Monday, which meant I had the whole weekend to sweat over it. I didn't do anything, I didn't go out. I was worried that I might not get the call, or that it would be like last time, when I was so near and yet so far. I couldn't sleep on Sunday night, and I was up early on Monday in case she rang first thing: I wanted to be fully awake and alert.

It was midday before the phone rang. I was upstairs, in my bedroom, and my mobile was lying on the table. When it rang I looked at the screen and it said 'Number withheld'. So I knew it wasn't Mum, or any of my friends. I took a massive gasp of air and picked it up. It was Sharon.

'We've got something to tell you. We want you to go into *Celebrity Big Brother*.'

I can't remember what I said but I think it was something like:

'God, what, are you joking?' Then I just said: 'Oh my God, oh my God.' I probably said it almost as many times as I did on the last night when I was waiting to leave the house!

Sharon must have thought I was nuts. When I put the phone down I screamed out loud: I was on my own in the house so nobody heard me. Then I put some music on,

Lionel Richie's 'All Night Long', really loud, and danced around my room for joy.

There was still a bit of me that couldn't believe it would actually happen.

But the dream was definitely back on, and I was more excited about it than I had ever been.

Chapter Six

Going In

It was Christmas 2005, and I was the happiest girl on the planet – but I couldn't share my news with anyone. I know I could have trusted Mum and Dean completely, but I didn't want to put the responsibility on them of having to keep absolutely quiet about what was about to happen.

It was a weird time, and the days passed in a blur. I kept telling myself I wouldn't be the only ordinary person going in, but I have to admit that I had a sneaking suspicion that it might just be me. Sharon and Sam, the researcher who looked after me, kept in touch – they were fantastic. I didn't ask them too many questions: I didn't want to put them in a position where they would have to lie to me.

When I was lined up for *Big Brother 6*, I'd been given a talk about the risks of telling anyone. They explained that you just tell one person, and that person just tells their best friend, who in turn tells just one more person. Before you know it, it's being talked about in the hairdresser's and the pub, and someone rings the newspapers. So I knew the risks, and it seemed doubly important this time as it was so unexpected that someone who wasn't a celebrity should be going in.

So I was really secretive. I didn't go out much, spending my time working out the clothes I wanted to take, booking my hair appointment, having a couple of sunbeds. Mum gave me some money, £300 – it was partly a loan and partly my Christmas present. I bought tracksuits, because I guessed we would be lying around a lot, skirts, tops and dresses. In a boutique in Southend I found a dress I really loved, so I bought it in black and in champagne. I always knew the pale one would be my eviction dress. I was not for one minute expecting to be in there for the full three weeks, but I still wanted to give myself lots of choices as to what to wear each day. I showed Mum what I had bought, and she loved the dress, but, funnily enough, she never asked me why I hadn't worn it over Christmas.

Mum didn't quiz me about what happened after the phone call from Sharon. She says she deliberately put it out of her mind, because she thought that if it was a disappointment for me, she would only be rubbing it in by asking about it.

My grandad was the only one who suspected anything – not that he had a clue what it was. But he did say to Mum, when he and Nan were over at our house on Boxing Day:

'That girl, she's always got a smile on her face, but there's something extra just now. It seems she's beaming all the time.'

Mum just thought it was because it was Christmas and New Year. Later Grandad said to me he couldn't work out why I was laughing so much, especially at things that weren't all that funny.

Mum wasn't surprised that I wasn't going out much, because she knows I'm not a clubbing person. She also knows I love family Christmases, with everyone around, doing daft things like trying to answer the questions on *Who Wants to Be a Millionaire?*.

Every morning when I woke up I would check the date on my mobile, and every day I was one day closer. It was so exciting. I bought the newspapers and read all the stories about who was predicted to be going into *Celebrity Big Brother*. Michael Barrymore's name dominated the headlines, and I could hardly believe there was a chance I would be in with him: I remembered watching *Strike It Lucky* with my mum when I was young, and to me he was a huge star. I also saw Faria Alam's name mentioned, and I was aware of her because of the scandal of her affair with Sven-Göran Eriksson, the England football manager. I didn't know Pete Burns, but he was also in the papers, tipped as a possible housemate.

New Year's Day was on a Sunday, so the next day was another bank holiday, with all the family at home. Gregg works in London for an insurance company, but he lives at home. He, Mum and Dean were all back at work on the Tuesday, and I spent the time packing and repacking my suitcase. I went to the hairdresser's and had some of my extensions replaced, and I had gel nails applied. (They came off within a week of being in the house. One pinged off, then another couple, so my hands looked weird and I took the rest off.)

I had no money, but I collected together a lot of copper and 5p pieces, which I loaded into a bag. I took the train to Southend to take all the loose change to one of those machines, in the entryway to a supermarket, which converts change into proper money. I figured I'd got maybe £15 – the bag was very heavy. But when I got there the machine hadn't been emptied and so it wasn't working. I was gutted. I could have cried my eyes out, because I wanted to buy another top, or some more make-up. And I then had to carry the heavy bag home!

I had a final sunbed the evening before I went in, and something terrible happened. The person who used the bed before me had obviously put hot tingle cream all over themselves, and there was enough left on the bed for my back to turn bright red. One of the girls from the salon wiped me down with a wet wipe, but I was so worried that the redness wouldn't disappear before I went into the house. Luckily, by the time I got home it had faded.

The day before I went in, I took out a bottle of champagne that we had left over from New Year.

When Mum came in from work I said: 'I've got something to tell you.'

She looked serious.

I just said: 'You're not going to believe it. I'm going into *Celebrity Big Brother* tomorrow.'

Mum sat down, then she stood up again, then she sat down again. Then she said: 'Is this for real, Chantelle?'

I told her it was, and we waited for Dean to come home

before cracking open the champagne. When Mum told him I had something to tell him, he thought I was pregnant!

I was able to be quite laid-back about it, because I'd had ages to get used to the idea. But it was a bombshell for them. They were in a state of shock, like I had been at first. It was:

'What? What? How can you be – it's for celebrities.'

It ended up with me spending the evening trying to calm them down. Mum couldn't face cooking dinner, so we phoned up for an Indian takeaway, but we were all too excited to eat much.

I decided not to tell Gregg or Dad, but I wrote notes for them and gave them to Mum to hand over once I was in the house.

For Gregg I wrote: 'Boo – surprise, hey? I bet this was a shock. Love you – and I'll be seeing you soon!'

For Dad I wrote: 'Dad – sorry I couldn't tell you about this, but it had to be kept a big secret. I love you and I'll see you soon, Chantelle.'

We talked until quite late, because I knew I wouldn't sleep much.

'You'll know I'm all right, but I won't know you are all right,' I said to Mum.

'Just enjoy yourself and don't worry about us,' she said.

We really thought I was only going to be in there for a few days, so we decided it would only be like me going away for a long weekend. I'd already done my packing, but Mum went through everything with me, just in case there was anything obvious that I'd forgotten.

Sam had rung me to say that she would be coming to

pick me up early the next day, Thursday 5 January. The programme wasn't on until the evening, when we would be filmed live going into the house, but they needed to have me (and, presumably, the others) at a hotel all day.

When she arrived at 7 a.m. and rang the doorbell, Gregg was in the downstairs shower at the back of the house, and I knew he would wonder what was going on as I'm not normally up at that time. I legged it downstairs.

'You can't come in, my brother's here,' I said to Sam. 'I'll be out in a few minutes.'

Then I ran back upstairs and shut my bedroom door. I listened until I heard Gregg go into his room and then I went downstairs. Mum and Dean were there – I think Dean, who normally left for work very early, stayed behind a bit to say goodbye to me.

I remember saying to him: 'Look after my mum for me, Dean.'

He said: 'I always look after your mum, Chantelle, but if it puts your mind at rest I promise to look after her extra well while you're away.'

Mum said: 'Clear your head of everything, forget about the rest of us. Go in and enjoy yourself.'

Then I grabbed my case quickly, before Gregg reappeared, and off I went, with Mum and Dean both saying 'Live the Dream' to me. They didn't shout it – they didn't want to alert Gregg. I felt a bit rotten not telling him or Dad, but I knew they'd find out soon enough.

It was winter, so it was still pitch dark at that time in the morning. The people carrier was outside, with Sam and a driver waiting for me. It was as we drove out of Wickford that it began to hit me. I remember thinking to myself: 'Oh, bloody hell, it really is happening!'

I wasn't nervous, just very excited. I had one worry though. Dad had to go to hospital that day, and I was quite concerned about him. He had been diagnosed with a second deep-vein thrombosis – the condition people sometimes get after long-haul air flights. It's a bit of an occupational risk of being a taxi driver, because you spend so much time sitting down. Plus he hadn't been doing as much exercise as he once did. He'd been put on warfarin, the blood-thinning medication, and he was going into hospital for a check-up that day.

I was worried, because I didn't know whether they would keep him in hospital. The idea of being in the house and not knowing what was happening with Dad was upsetting. Mum had promised me that she would be the one who would decide if anything in the outside world was important enough for me to be pulled out of the house, and I completely trusted her. She'd reassured me that if anything was seriously wrong with Dad, she'd make sure Big Brother told me.

The driver dropped me and Sam at a hotel – I've no idea where – and when we checked into the room Sam told me I would have to hand over my phone at midday. I rang Dad, but he texted that he was at the hospital and couldn't call me back. So I sent him a text saying: 'Whatever happens, Dad, I love you.'

When he read it, apparently he thought: 'Blimey, does she know something I don't?'

We are very close, and I'm always telling him I love him,

but I wouldn't normally send him a text like that. Sam gave me permission to keep my phone switched on long enough for him to call me back after he had left the hospital with the all-clear – that was all I wanted to know. I told him again that I loved him, and he said later he wondered why I was going so OTT. He kept asking me if I was all right – he must have suspected something was going on, but he had no idea what.

I also rang Mum and she wished me good luck. I knew that she and Dean would be there when I walked into the house that evening. In fact, Mum took the afternoon off work, and she found it really hard to tell a lie to her boss about why she wanted the extra time. She said she was going out somewhere special, and needed time to get ready. That was true – but she didn't say where she was going. (The next day, when everyone knew, and all the staff from the offices nearby came in to see her, her boss commented that she thought Mum had brushed her off a bit when she asked where she was going.)

Sam was a great girl to spend the day with. She had to check all my belongings and pack them into the official *BB* suitcase, writing down everything I had brought. Apparently I'd packed as many clothes as most people do when they go in for the full-length *Big Brother*! I had too much jewellery, and I had to take out a couple of necklaces and some earrings. This time I had also packed a couple of bottles of wine, as my luxury item.

I wasn't allowed to watch TV, but Sam had a stash of videos, so we watched some films and just chatted. I ordered a big lunch – cod, chips and mushy peas – because

I wasn't sure when I would next get a decent meal. I still didn't know I was the only non-celebrity, although for some unknown reason I suspected it.

It's hard to explain how surreal and weird that day was: on one level I could believe what was happening to me, and on another it all seemed like a dream, and I would soon wake up and find myself back in the real world.

There had been no talk of any payment for my time in *Big Brother*, and I certainly didn't expect or want any. But that day, before I went in, there was 8p in my bank account, I still had debts, and I had no plans for a job when I came out. Yet that was all as far as possible from my mind: all I could think about was the next few hours.

Because Endemol, the TV company, were donating some of the proceeds from the voting phone lines to charity, all the celebrities were asked to nominate a charity for their share to go to. I chose Breast Cancer Care. I don't know anyone who has had breast cancer, but it is something that affects so many women around the world, so I thought it would be an ideal choice.

At about 4 p.m. the driver came back and took Sam and me to Elstree. When we got near to the studio I had to wear a white mask over the whole of my face, with just two slits for my eyes, in case I was spotted by any photographers. Not that they would have recognised me, but I was already being treated like a celebrity. It was like a military operation getting in there: the driver was talking to someone on his radio, and when we got near the gates I was told to lie down. I could see the flashes of light from the cameras as the paparazzi tried to get snatch photos of this 'celebrity' who was being whisked in.

I wasn't allowed to take the mask off until I was hidden away in a dressing room, just like when I had gone in as a guinea pig. There was nothing to do: no phone, TV, music or anything to read. I wasn't hungry, but I ate some sweets and chocolate. Time dragged, and I longed for it to be nine o'clock. At 6 p.m. I knew Mum and Dean were being picked up to be brought to the studio, and after that it was *really* weird, knowing they were close to me, possibly somewhere along the same corridor, maybe just through the wall in the room next door.

I could have invited more people to see me go in, and I did think about asking some friends. But I worried so much about the possibility of a leak, that in the end it was safer to keep it just to Mum and Dean. I told Mum to ring Gregg at twenty to nine, because I knew he was going round to Dad's flat that night for a meal. I also asked her to ring Nan and Grandad, and just tell them to watch Channel 4. But Mum was told she had to switch her phone off, so she couldn't.

She and Dean were actually locked into the green room, the hospitality suite. According to Mum, Dean couldn't sit down the whole time. Mum wasn't worried.

'She'll be all right,' she said to Dean. 'I know she's got confidence, and it's something she so much wants to do.'

But even so, she said that her stomach turned over when the show began, and when she heard Davina say my name. They weren't allowed to join the crowd outside, so they watched me going in on TV. They could have done that at home, but Mum wouldn't have missed being there for the world! She told me afterwards that when she first saw me on the screen she just wanted to reach out and touch me.

About half an hour before I went in I got changed. The pink jogging bottoms and top I had been wearing all day were added to my suitcase, and I put on the black, drop-waisted lacy dress, the same as the champagne-coloured one I had chosen for leaving the house. I don't suppose many viewers realised I wore the same dress going in and coming out, just in different colours. It was cold, so I also wore a short jacket, more of a shrug really, in black fake fur with a diamanté clip at the front. I had bought it from Dorothy Perkins just a couple of weeks earlier.

Finally, after what seemed like an eternity to me, it was quarter to nine. Phil and Sharon came to see me.

'There's something funny going on here,' I said. 'What have you got on the back burner?'

They just laughed and didn't really answer, and I didn't want to press them. First of all, I knew they wouldn't tell me, and secondly, I didn't want to put them in a position of having to lie to me. I like them both, much more than just as producers of *Big Brother*, they're just lovely people. Then they both wished me luck, and said, 'See you soon!' I'm sure neither of them suspected it would be another three weeks before we met again.

At five to nine I was taken to the door of the studio building and fitted with my microphone. There was a slight delay, then I climbed into the limo with Sam. The *BB* music was playing in the car, but for some reason I also had to put headphones on. There was a countdown, and then off we went.

It was only a short drive, and then the limo was pulling up and Sam was opening the door to let me out. It was incredible: there were masses of people there, huge cheers. Just before I got out of the car the driver turned to me and said: 'Go on, girl, you go for it.'

It was really nice of him, and I remembered his words once or twice when things weren't easy in the house.

I'd been told beforehand what to expect, but it was still mind-blowing. I walked towards two banks of photographers, who were all calling my name. I remember thinking:

'How do they know my name?'

I waved to them and posed for them, loving every minute. There was a security man walking a few feet behind me, and he followed me up the red carpet. Then I was on my own climbing the steps, into the famous house. I wasn't nervous: I'd lived and relived the scene in my head, ever since I first knew I was going in. I'd fantasised about climbing out of the limo and the cheers and flashes, so it didn't daunt me at all.

I had no idea, until I saw the video after I came out, what the viewers were seeing or hearing. But I know now that Davina opened the show with:

'One house, ten celebrities, eleven housemates. Welcome to *Celebrity Big Brother 2006*. I can tell you there are more than ever before, they will be locked away for longer than ever before, a full twenty-three days, and Big Brother is going to be as twisted and evil as ever.

'Tonight, eleven housemates are moving in. But only ten are celebrities. The first housemate who will enter the house is a nobody. And the only way they will get to stay is if they can convince the rest of the house that they are, in fact, famous.

'But Big Brother hasn't told them that yet, so shhhh, it's a secret . . .'

The first part of the show also included a tour of the house. Then there was an ad break, and after that Davina said:

'Before we meet our celebrities we have to put our very special housemate Number One into the house. Back in February last year *Big Brother* toured Britain and Ireland looking for housemates. Thousands auditioned. *Big Brother* selected just one of them to put in the *Celebrity Big Brother* house. Lucky thing! Or is she? Would you like to meet housemate Number One?'

Then they played my video.

'Hiya,' I said, 'my name is Chantelle. I'm twenty-two, I'm a model and promotions girl and I'm from Essex. I'd describe myself as fun, a bit dizzy, outrageous. People's first impressions of me are lip gloss, bleached hair, fake tan, make-up, giggly.

'I wouldn't mind being in there with Brad Pitt or someone like that. Perhaps the Chippendales? Just me and the Chippendales, that would do nicely.

'I'm not like a person who would run over and go "Oh my God" just because someone is a celebrity. They breathe the same air as us, at the end of the day, don't they? I'll treat them the same as anybody else.

'What makes me sad is people arguing. Nobody seems to have any morals these days. I don't like lies. I can't lie. You can see from my face when I'm lying.'

Davina then talked about me, as the cameras showed me sashaying up the walkway to the steps. When I look at the video, even I am surprised at how confident I look.

Davina said: 'Chantelle still lives at home with her mum and stepdad in Essex. Her favourite food is Mexican, and her proudest moment was winning Majorette of the Year. She got into the last twelve of the Miss Greater London competition, and she has a phobia about spiders. She goes for a sunbed once a week and tops up her fake tan every two days, and her favourite colour is pink.'

I had no idea what was being said: all I could hear was the cheering of the crowd. I never saw Davina, or heard her voice. I turned and waved and blew kisses at everyone. Then the doors slid open and I was inside. When they closed, the noise was shut out, and, finally, after a long wait, I was a housemate – and the madness had begun.

I've since talked to the rest of my family about what happened the night I went in. Gregg and Dad had just finished their steak-and-chips dinner and Dad was flicking around through the TV channels, trying to find something to watch. Thank God there wasn't an Arsenal match on, or they'd have never seen my big arrival.

Anyway, Dad switched to Channel 4 and they both heard my name. Dad had already flicked over with the remote, but as soon as it registered they went straight back and saw me going in through the door.

'I can't believe she's doing this to me – what will my mates say?' Gregg said, apparently.

Then both their phones started ringing, as everyone called to make sure they weren't missing it.

Nan switched over when I was in the house, standing by the sink.

'What's she doing on the screen?' she said to Grandad. She thought I might be there as a hostess, to hand out drinks to the celebrities when they went in!

Chapter Seven

Kandy Floss (with a K!)

The house looked almost like I had remembered it: the colours were the same, the layout of the furniture was the same. But it seemed starker, brighter. I'd forgotten just how strong the lights are (they have to be, for the cameras) and it was eerily quiet. I hadn't been told I was going in first, but I'd suspected I'd be one of the early arrivals, because I'd gone in so soon after 9 p.m., when the TV show started.

But what do you do when there's nothing to do – and the eyes of millions of viewers are on you?

'Warm welcome!' I said, out loud. 'Where is everyone? Hi! Come on, you're hiding!!'

The only reply came from Big Brother.

'Would Chantelle come to the Diary Room?'

'Course I will.'

I knew where it was. There was a large envelope on the seat of the famous Diary Room chair, a big circular blue chair trimmed with yellow, and with more than enough room for two people (as we would find out later!). I sat down, and had my first mind-blowing conversation with BB.

'How are you, Chantelle?'

'Very well. Ecstatic.'

'As you know, this is *Celebrity Big Brother*, and you are not a celebrity.'

'You got that right!'

'You were told that there would be a mixture of celebrities and non-celebrities in the *Big Brother* house. In fact, you will be the only housemate who is not a celebrity.'

Although I'd half expected it, it made my heart race.

'Oooooh! What's the catch?' I asked, still feeling that BB had something else up his sleeve for me.

'In order to stay in the *Big Brother* house, you must earn celebrity status.'

'OK.'

'To do that, you must complete a secret mission. Chantelle, your mission is to convince the other celebrities that you are a genuine celebrity. If you succeed, you will have earned the right to stay in the *Celebrity Big Brother* house. If you fail, you will be evicted. Do you understand?'

I said I did, but the full implications hadn't hit me. Then Big Brother told me I was not allowed to impersonate any existing celebrity.

'What? Oh my God!'

I think that was the first of the many, many times I

would say 'Oh my God' over the next three weeks. Then I had to open the envelope, which had the details about my new role. As everyone now knows, I had to pretend to be a singer in a girl band called Kandy Floss (with a K!) and that my band's biggest hit single was called 'I Want It Right Now'.

'It's a deal,' I told BB.

I think lots of people would have been really thrown by it. I've got no acting experience, I'd only ever been in a school play. I didn't think I could convince anyone that I really was a pop star, but I thought: 'For God's sake. I've waited so long and I'm finally here, so even though it's completely ridiculous, I'm going to go for it.'

All I asked was whether the band was still around at the moment. BB told me it was, and that I could make up any details I needed, but I must stick to the name Kandy Floss (with a K!)

'Shame no one's ever heard of it!' I said.

I left the Diary Room and wandered around the room, repeating to myself the name of the band and the song. It suddenly hit me: there were bound to be some other housemates with a background in the music business. I remembered Mark Owen and Bez from other *Celebrity Big Brothers*. How would I deal with questions about going on tour or being in a recording studio and all those things bands do?

Oh my God!

I seemed to be on my own for ages, but it was actually only a few minutes. I remember really wanting to phone Mum, because I'd told her that I thought something weird was going on. I wanted to say: 'See, I told you something was going to happen.'

Then the door opened and Michael Barrymore walked in. It was the weirdest thing, to be with someone I'd watched on telly for so many years. It was pretty surreal. I could tell he was a bit emotional, because he'd been cheered all the way in and – after all the things that had happened to him – he'd found the crowd support very moving.

After we'd kissed and said our names he asked me where I was from. I instantly replied that I was from a girl band called Kandy Floss.

'I know that. But where are you from?' he said.

He meant, where did I live. But it was interesting that he'd pretended to know me as a celeb – my first little victory! But I wasn't smug, because I knew Michael had been living in New Zealand and probably wouldn't be up to date with every girl band who had made it to a low position in the charts.

The next person to come in was Pete Burns, who used to be with the band Dead or Alive. I didn't know him, but I'd seen his picture in the papers in the last few days, when he was tipped to be one of the housemates. Just as well, because I don't think I would have known whether he was a man or a woman if I hadn't read about him. He looked amazing.

He was a bit tougher to handle than Michael. He said he'd never heard of Kandy Floss, but added, 'I've not been in England for a while.' He asked me how many girls were in the band and off the top of my head I said five (later on,

I wished I'd said four, or even three, because there would have been fewer names to remember). He also asked about my record, and what the band were doing now.

'We're just working on stuff,' I said.

Luckily, before he could ask any more, Traci Bingham arrived. I remembered *Baywatch* a bit, but I couldn't specifically remember Traci. In quick succession the others came in: Maggot from Goldie Lookin' Chain and the actress Rula Lenska were the next two, and I'd never heard of either of them, although I'd heard of Maggot's band.

Then Jodie Marsh walked in, and inside me a small panic button was pressed. Jodie comes from Essex, not too far away from where I live, and I've actually been in clubs at the same time she was there. I know her brother slightly – well, I've chatted to him. I was really worried that she would remember me as just another face in the crowd, rather than as a real celebrity.

But we got chatting straight away, and she didn't show any sign of recognition. We both agreed we had no idea who Rula was.

Dennis Rodman came in next. I hadn't a clue about him, either. He was enormous, with his face covered in piercings and loads of tattoos all over his body. I didn't have time to feel overawed by him, I was too busy introducing myself to people and trying to make sure I kept my story straight.

Faria was the next in, and I knew who she was. There had been so much in the papers about her when she had her affair with Sven-Göran Eriksson, but there had also been plenty of speculation that she would be one of the housemates.

The next to come in was Preston, and my memories are such a blur that I can't recollect our first meeting. One of the amazing things that anyone who lives in the *Big Brother* house has, when they come out, is the chance to relive what happened on video. It's also an astonishing chance to hear what other people say about you behind your back – something you just never know about in real life. It's very, very weird, and you learn things you had no idea about at the time. People who seemed to be nice to each other were actually bitching away like mad behind their backs.

It has been a real eye-opener for me: I think I learned more about human nature in those three weeks than I have in the rest of my twenty-three-year life!

Looking back at Preston's little video introduction of himself (which, of course, I knew nothing about at the time), he said he thought he would be good at sitting around doing nothing in the house, because, on tour with his band Ordinary Boys, 'I've spent two years of my life sitting in a transit van staring into space.' He also said he was 'looking forward to sharing a bedroom with some sexy girls!'

I shook hands with him when we met, but we didn't say much. He and Maggot knew each other, from both being in bands. All I could think was: these are two who will suss me, so I've got to keep away from them.

The final housemate to arrive was George Galloway, the MP. I had no idea who he was, I'm ashamed to say. I'd never heard his name or seen his face before – politics isn't something I've paid much attention to.

Then we were all in. I remember thinking that it was like the guinea-pig run, with lots of complete strangers around me, even if some of them had very familiar faces.

I couldn't remember their names. My head was too full, what with remembering my own new life as part of a girl band. I also had to pretend I didn't know my way around the house, that it was as new to me as it was to all the others.

I have to admit, though, that even in those early minutes, I glanced across and saw Preston standing in the kitchen area, and I thought to myself that he had a really cute face. But I had no intention of going across and chatting to him – he, along with Maggot and Pete, were the ones I didn't want to spend any time with in case they caught me out.

At one point, when I was talking to Preston later, he asked me a question about the band. I was running the hot water at the kitchen sink, so I pretended I'd burnt my finger, just to get out of answering the question.

When we were all in, George immediately took control and proposed a toast to 'a happy and harmonious time'. Funny when you think he would later do more than anyone to disrupt the harmony!

After we'd gone round the circle saying who we were, he commented: 'Well. We're not short of singers.'

I think that was the first time it flashed through my mind that I might be asked to sing. I pushed the thought away – I can't sing! Anyone who knows me will tell you that.

But on that first night, singing wasn't my biggest worry.

I took the first opportunity that I could to go to the Diary Room and talk to *BB*.

I said: 'Houston, we have a problem. I've got no problem with faking it, and I think I'm doing a good job. But Jodie is from Brentwood, and I've been to pubs and clubs and seen her out and I think she recognises me. I'm sure she's seen me, and she may know I'm not in a girl band. If anyone's going to get me, it will be her.

'If she questions me I'll tell her I've done modelling and bits and pieces but now I'm in a band.'

BB asked me what I thought of my new identity.

I said: 'Loving it! I'm a ready-made pop star, and I haven't even done anything to get here. I'm loving it. I'm up there with the celebs, in't I?'

Through being in the Diary Room I was the last to go into the bedroom, so I didn't have any choice of bed. I ended up sandwiched between Dennis, who snored loudly and talked in his sleep, and Pete. George also snored a lot, and Michael did occasionally.

I made one of my famous gaffes that night – well, they became famous, because the press picked up on them and made a big thing, trying to make me out as a dumb blonde, I suppose. But as I later said, 'I know I'm not blonde, and I know I'm not dumb.'

Michael told everyone he was a gynaecologist. He was just fooling around, but I believed him. I asked what a gynaecologist was, but it wasn't as dumb a question as it sounds: I knew it was a kind of doctor. I thought that maybe while he was away in New Zealand he had retrained for a new job.

Anyway, when I asked my dumb question Michael said: 'I love you, I've fallen in love with you.'

I had the feeling I was doing well with my acting. When Preston and Jodie went into the Diary Room together they admitted they had never heard of George or Rula.

Preston said: 'Who's that girl in Kit Kat, Kandy Floss or whatever? I haven't heard of them – but I'm sure some of the others haven't heard of me.'

I think everyone went into the Diary Room on that first night, and of course I had no idea what any of them said, until I saw the videos later. But I already knew that Pete had a very sharp, witty tongue. I could never take him seriously, not even when he was being very bitchy. This is what he told Big Brother about the house:

'The house is vile, it's not my taste. It looks like a bad LSD trip to IKEA. But I didn't expect heaven with harps playing . . .' I didn't hear him say it, of course, but when I heard it on the video it made me smile: it's very Pete.

Sitting outside with Maggot, I told him a long joke. I think I did it to stop him talking to me about my pop career. Anyway, it was a story about a dog, and it went on and on before we got to the punchline. I really wound him in.

'I didn't know we had another comedian in the house,' he said. It was a joke that Dean told me, and for a moment I thought about him and Mum.

It's funny being in there, you do lose track of the outside world. I'd have flashes of thinking about them: I could look at the clock on the cooker and work out where Mum would be and what she would be doing. After a few days I would really start to miss her, very badly. But at the beginning, it's surprising how easy it is to cut off from life outside, and to forget that you are on camera.

When I finally went to bed, at about half past two, I had to put up with Dennis trying to chat me up. He said that by the fourth day we would be sleeping together.

In normal life I would have told him to get lost, but I didn't want to cause any dramas and draw attention to myself, so I turned over and went to sleep. I was so exhausted after a very long day that I did get to sleep quite easily, despite all the excitement.

Waking up the next day was wicked. I lay in bed and thought: 'It's true, it's not a dream. I'm really here.'

I genuinely thought I was doing well with my act – I had no idea that some of the others were suspicious of me. I'd chatted with both Preston and George, and when they asked me about where my 'hit' single made it in the charts, I said 58. But I also told George it got to 47 in Germany. I was making it all up – Big Brother didn't give me any help.

It was Preston who kicked off everyone else's suspicions. He was talking to George and Faria.

'The kid with Kandy Floss – I haven't heard of that group,' he said.

Faria said she hadn't, either.

George said: 'She told me she had one hit and it was number 47 in the charts.'

Preston said: '58.'

'I thought she said 47,' said George.

'You don't think she's a red herring?' Preston asked. 'No,

I'm being really suspicious. I don't want to be a paranoid idiot.'

They carried on discussing it, with George swearing that I said 47, because he apparently commented that it was good to have made the Top 50. They agreed it was odd that Preston, who knows the chart scene, has never heard of Kandy Floss.

'But if she is a struggling musician I'll feel bad for being paranoid,' he said.

Faria volunteered to ask me outright – but she never did.

I was blissfully unaware of all this, and actually felt I was doing well. I stupidly relaxed and had two glasses of champagne when they were being handed round that morning. It was pretty silly, considering I had to be on my guard all the time to remember my cover story.

But it turned out to be even more silly when Big Brother called me to the Diary Room and announced that there would be a quiz that afternoon, and that the questions would be about the housemates' fields of expertise and their life history.

I remember sinking my head in my hands as BB reeled off the names of the other girls in my 'band', and I cursed myself for making it such a big group. But I've got a good memory, and in a strange way the champagne probably helped by making me more relaxed. If you ask me now the names of Kandy Floss, and of our three hit singles, and how I came to join the band, I can still tell you.

From the Diary Room I went into the bedroom, where it was quiet, and drilled the names into my head. I have a friend called Emma, so I remembered her, and I know two girls, one called Natalie and one Michelle, so that helped with those two. I was worried about remembering Kelly, then I thought of Kelly Brook. I found it a bit trickier remembering the name of my 'cousin' Kate, who I was with in my previous band.

I was on edge the rest of the day, until we had the quiz late in the afternoon. I really wanted to do well, because it was obvious the whole event was staged around me. If I didn't do well, or manage to say a lot about my band, I figured Big Brother would be evil and make me do more tests.

When it came to it, I did OK. I can remember Michael Barrymore, the quizmaster, giving the other team the right answer to one of the questions about me, and I was really wanting to tell them myself – I was so proud to know the answers! But also, I wanted to get Big Brother off my back.

But even though I did well, the suspicions continued. We had a party after the quiz, and late that night I found myself in the spa with Preston and Traci. Maybe I was getting a bit more confident, or maybe it was because I'd had a drink, but I wasn't avoiding Preston as much as I had been. He took the opportunity to question me:

'I thought you might be making it up because I've never heard of you. Well, not you, but I thought Big Brother might be making it up.'

I just said, 'No.'

He carried on: 'Maybe it's Big Brother's little thing? But it's not true? You are in a proper band?'

'We've been together since 2002 . . .'

'Promise?'

'What?'

'Promise on your mother's life.'

My stomach churned. But I instantly had a picture in my head of Mum shouting at the television screen, telling me to say it. I crossed my fingers and my toes under the water and said:

'I swear on my mother's life. Scout's honour . . .'

I knew Mum would understand. She'd have been more upset if I refused to swear on her life, and then got evicted. If I hadn't done it, she would have gone mental with me. Anyway, it's only some old superstition, and I don't really believe it, and neither does she. But I was upset for a couple of days because of it, and I cried in bed that night. The worst thing was not being able to talk to her, and tell I didn't mean it.

After that, Traci joined our conversation, and Preston told her that he had wondered if my band really existed.

I said: 'You'll know all about us when we get out . . .' And I reckon that was one of the true things I said, among my lies.

Before we went to bed, another housemate heard something that must have upset him. Jodie was talking to me and Traci and Faria in the kitchen about Michael. Unbeknown to her, he was listening at the door. It was an event that would upset the house a great deal, in the days to come. I don't know how much he was able to hear, but from that time on, he really didn't seem to like Jodie at all.

But perhaps the oddest thing that happened that day – and I didn't know about it until I was out of the house – was when George went into the Diary Room and was asked about his fellow housemates. This is what he said about me:

'Chantelle is surely the youngest in the group, if not in age then definitely in maturity. She's a little girl, and a very sweet one. She is a girl who has begun to make it in the music industry. She may not have a glittering career ahead of her. But for now, she's LIVING THE DREAM.'

I can't believe he used that phrase, I definitely hadn't said it in the house.

But he was dead right about one thing: I *was* living the dream.

Chapter Eight

I'm a Real Celebrity

I already liked Preston, but I was still very nervous about talking to him, especially now I knew he had suspicions. And for most of the next day, I wasn't up to much conversation with anyone. But Big Brother really put me to the test.

We were told that, in order to get the full 'luxury shopping budget', we all had to give a performance of what we were famous for. My heart sank – and so did the hearts of all my family on the outside. Dad said that when he saw my face after the task was announced, he wanted to leap into the telly and give me a cuddle. He'd been really worried about me having to tell lies anyway – he knows I'm a bad liar, and that I giggle when I'm not telling the truth. But I'm a giggly person anyway, so I think the other housemates just accepted it.

But to be told I was going to have to sing! Mum, Dean,

Dad, Gregg – in fact, anyone who has ever heard me sing – were sure this would be testing me too far. Dean kept telling Mum not to worry because 'lots of these real pop singers can't hit a note'. What they, and I, didn't realise was that I would be allowed to sing along to my own 'record' – in other words, I'd have music and other voices to keep me going.

Big Brother told me about the task, in the Diary Room.

I said: 'Oh my God! I can't believe this. I can't believe you have done this to me. I can't sing, but they think I'm a lead singer in a band, so I can't even make the excuse that I'm one of the backing girls or whatever you call them. This is going to be the most cringeworthy thing I've ever done in my life. This is a joke. Have you ever heard how a cat sings?'

I had to practise 'I Want It Right Now' in the Diary Room with headphones on, and I was worried it would be broadcast to the nation. My first impression, when I heard my own 'hit', was that it was a pretty catchy song with good words. If I'd known at the time that it was written by a very well-established songwriter, Colin Campsie, who has penned hits for the Spice Girls and Natalie Imbruglia, and that it was originally written with Kylie Minogue in mind, I think I would have been even more freaked out. I'm glad I didn't find out until much later.

What I didn't realise, as I tried to get my head round the lyrics and the tune, was that the other housemates could hear enough to know I was singing.

'Singing? Is that what you call it?' Pete said. If I'd heard him say it, I'd have laughed my head off and agreed with him.

I didn't want them to wonder about why I was in there so long, so I came out, with a copy of the lyrics of the song. Maggot had the lyrics of his song as well, so it didn't look too bad.

I took the wordsheet into the bedroom and put it on the bed, and then tried to glance at it without looking as though I was reading it. Pete was in there.

I told him: 'It just won't sound the same, doing it on my own. There's a bit I don't usually sing – the other girls sing it.' I was trying to prepare him for the worst.

Before we had to perform I had a glass of wine, to help me relax and keep myself chilled out. But I was acting so hysterical that Preston thought I'd had a lot to drink. I was walking about, pacing up and down, giggling even more than usual, psyching myself up for the task.

I didn't want to be the first to perform, but I didn't want to be the last – I figured if I was last, my performance would be what they all remembered. Luckily for me, I was called to do my act third, after Maggot and George.

I was wearing an orange dress with a really short skirt, and what with having to keep pulling it down with one hand, and holding the microphone and the lyrics in the other, it was all a bit complicated. But the wine definitely helped, because I got into it and danced up and down the 'stage' area as I sang it. I lost my place with the music once, but I really felt I'd got away with it, because they all clapped and cheered afterwards. How little I knew!

I sat down feeling I'd given a wicked performance. I was

in a bit of a daze, and I didn't really notice the other acts. The rest of that evening was a bit of a blur. I wasn't actually shaking outside, but inside I was. I clapped and cheered everyone else, but I wasn't watching them too closely.

The only person I could share my feeling of triumph with was Big Brother, and in the Diary Room I really let my excitement show.

'Hey, check me out! Famous pop star!'

I said I thought the performance had gone really well.

'I'm proud of myself, I've never even done karaoke except when I was maybe eleven, I would never stand up in a pub and sing, yet I've just stood up there not just singing for a laugh but pretending to be a famous pop star in front of them. I am proud of myself, really, really proud.'

Big Brother asked me if I thought my performance had aroused any suspicions.

'Nope, not at all,' I answered honestly.

They say ignorance is bliss, and I'm glad I was ignorant about what the others were really thinking.

Jodie told Maggot and Preston: 'You've made me paranoid about Chantelle not being real. I hadn't thought about it until you said and then I watched the performance and it was like she really didn't know her own song. I studied her closely and it was like not only did she not know the words but sometimes she didn't know when to come in with the music.'

In another part of the house, George and Rula were also on my case.

George said: 'Even the little girl, Chantelle, I didn't

believe she was a pop star. I thought, there's something funny here.'

Rula agreed. 'I still don't believe it. She turned her back on the audience, which I found strange. Although she did come to life in a way I hadn't seen before.'

Then George got back on to the subject of me giving different positions in the charts to him and Preston.

'If you're not telling the truth, it's hard to remember the lies you've told,' he said.

Funnily enough, Preston, who kicked off all the suspicion about me, was now convinced I was telling the truth.

'I was really suspicious of Chantelle,' he said in the Diary Room. 'A lot of things didn't add up. I thought her band wasn't real and you put her in here to pretend she was a celebrity, and that she is just an actress. But I'm over that now, so it's all right.'

Evidently, my performance convinced somebody!

But if I thought that was a tough challenge, worse was to come. The next day was my big test, and on it hung my future in the house.

We all had an inkling that something was afoot, and one of the others had mentioned that there might be a live television show that day. It was a bit scary – *Big Brother* is normally only live for evictions, and I honestly did think I could be walking out that evening.

Introducing the show, Davina said: 'For four days, promotions girl Chantelle has been hobnobbing with the stars. But this is where it gets serious. Housemates must rate themselves in order of fame. If they rate Chantelle the least famous person in the house, then she has failed. If she is not the lowest, then she stays.'

Of course, in the house we didn't hear any of that. But we knew what we had to do, because George read out the task details.

'Housemates, today's task is for a very, very special reward. In the garden are eleven podiums, numbered one to eleven. Housemates must rank themselves in order of fame. Housemates must decide among themselves which podium each stands on. You have a maximum of two minutes.'

It was raining outside, and we'd all been issued with warm puffa jackets and umbrellas. I remember standing in front of the cooker to block everyone's view of the clock (the only clock we had in there was on the cooker) so they wouldn't be reminded of the possibility of it being live. I was very warm standing there, but I stuck it out. If they'd noticed it was a few minutes to nine they would probably have realised it was a live show, and wondered why.

When the klaxon sounded and we went outside, I was saved by the fact that they all started to argue about who should be in the top slot. Jodie thought it should be Dennis, as he is more famous around the world, but George thought it should be Michael, because this was a British show. We wasted so much time on that, and we only had two minutes, so at the end the rest of us just had to grab a podium.

Maggot had gone to number 11 straight away. He's naturally modest: when he first walked into the house he introduced himself by saying, 'I'm just here to make up the numbers.' So when the one-minute warning went, and we knew we had to hurry, he jumped up there. I was just hanging around at the back. I had no idea, of course, but Mum and Dean had come up for the live show, and they were screaming at the big TV screen in the hospitality room.

'Get on a podium! Get on, Chantelle!'

They were so excited that one of the researchers said that the cameras ought to be in there, as it was even more riveting than what was happening on screen.

I made a move towards number 10, then I edged along to number 9. Preston stood on number 10.

Perhaps he and Maggot were just being very nice to me, or perhaps they had genuinely accepted that I was a celebrity. More likely, they simply didn't want to fail the task and lose the promised reward.

When I look back at the video of those few moments, my face looks frozen. I really was terrified I wasn't going to manage it. And then, when I stood up there, it flashed through my mind that maybe Maggot was going to be evicted instead of me: perhaps, by winning my secret task, I'd pushed him out. I was quite upset.

Once it was over, we all trooped back inside. Some of the others were complaining that they couldn't see the point of the task, but I knew completely what it was all about. It was all about me!

Soon after we went back inside I was called to the Diary Room. There, on the chair, was champagne and chocolates and other goodies, including a poster of me. I said – can't you guess? – 'Oh my God!'

Then Big Brother spoke:

'Chantelle, as you know, you entered the house as a non-celebrity, a nobody. There is no such band as Kandy Floss. Since entering, you have been on a secret mission to achieve celebrity status. Tonight you have convinced the rest of the house that you are more famous than Preston or Maggot.'

I said: 'That's fantastic, brilliant. I've passed my mission. I'm not exactly famous – I just passed a secret mission, didn't I?'

Big Brother said: 'Do you think you will be accepted by your fellow housemates?'

As he asked that question, I had a funny feeling that perhaps the others were watching. I remembered from previous *Big Brothers* that it is possible to feed the broadcast from the Diary Room on to a screen in the house, and I sensed that was happening.

I said: 'If they are watching this, I hope they understand how much pressure I've had put on me. Also, I hope they put themselves in my place. Like you said, I'm a nobody, and I hope they think back to the time when they were nobody, and if they had the chance I had, find it in themselves to think they would have done exactly the same thing as me.'

I wanted to explain to them, and tell them I was sorry for lying.

Then Big Brother asked me if I would consider releasing my record, 'I Want It Right Now'.

'If they put a voice over mine!' I said, giggling.

Finally, Big Brother asked me for an autograph. I thought it was a wind-up.

I said: 'Oh, shut up. You're taking the mick.'

I thought it was a trick. I couldn't think how, but it seemed a bit odd.

When I came out of the Diary Room, everyone was waiting to mob me with hugs and kisses. Preston was first, and

'You swore on your mother's life!' he teased me.

All I could say was, 'Sorry, sorry, sorry . . .' I felt really, really happy to have it out in the open, and so proud of myself to have passed my test. As far as I was concerned, I was already a *Big Brother* winner, just to have got through this day when I could have been evicted.

Instead of packing my things and moving out, we had a party, with a pink tablecloth, lots to eat and drink, balloons and a Polaroid camera to take crazy pictures of ourselves. *BB* even played 'I Want It Right Now', and we all danced to it.

I tried to speak to all of them individually, to say how sorry I was for lying. I told Jodie that I thought she was the one most likely to have sussed me. I genuinely didn't get any feeling that any of them resented me for tricking them, or for being in the house under false pretences. I was worried they would think I had made fools out of them, but even Preston and Maggot, who were rated less famous than me, thought it was funny.

George told me they were all thrilled for me, and Jodie said she and Preston had agreed that they didn't care if I was fake because they liked me.

It was brilliant to be able to relax, not to have to be on my guard all the time in case I said the wrong thing and gave myself away. Traci made me laugh when she asked if

I had been telling the truth about being a vegetarian – did she think I'd invented it to increase my celebrity status?

After a few drinks, Jodie, Preston and I went into the Diary Room to thank Big Brother for a brilliant party. Big Brother asked Preston to elaborate on the suspicions he's had about me, and Jodie chipped in:

Preston: 'I thought, "I've never heard of her, there's something not right about it." '

Jodie: 'Then you told me and that set me off, and I was annoyed because it made me well paranoid.'

Preston: 'George kept going on. I thought I was being a bit paranoid, as she swore on her mother's life. Which she did . . .'

Even though I was pissed, I realised I had an opportunity to let Mum know how difficult that had been for me.

'I know my mum understood,' I said, 'and I had my fingers crossed, lots of things crossed. Mum, I love you!'

I was thrilled later to find that my message to Mum was broadcast. You are not supposed to send messages to the outside world, but I think *Big Brother* knew how much it meant to me. I know it made Mum cry.

Big Brother then asked Preston: 'How does it feel to be less famous than Chantelle?'

We all screamed with laughter.

Then Preston said: 'I couldn't be less famous than a more fantastic girl.'

I turned and planted a big kiss on his cheek, leaving a lipstick imprint. Preston turned to show it to the camera.

'I'll never wash again,' he said.

It was the first time I'd kissed him, and it didn't mean

anything. It was just a peck on the cheek. But I already knew that I liked being around him, that he and Jodie were my best friends in there. It was silly, flirty, funny. Obviously, Jodie hadn't recognised me from the pubs and clubs where I had seen her, so all my fears about that had been unnecessary, and we had a laugh about it later.

It then got even sillier. I was in the bedroom with Preston and Maggot, all on one bed together having a 9, 10 and 11 group hug (we were the ones who came 9, 10 and 11 in the line-up) when Jodie and Pete piled in on top of us. Poor old Maggot was nearly suffocated by Jodie's boobs. It was all ridiculous, but we'd had loads to drink. For me, too, it was my first chance to let myself go.

I was so tired I fell asleep easily that night. But I woke up early the next day and lay there in the dark feeling really happy. I hugged myself with joy. I felt it was a great victory for me, over all the modelling disappointments and everything else that had not gone well for me. I had finally proved that if I wanted to do something, I could achieve it. I kept thinking about Mum, and how proud she would be.

For me, the whole focus of those first four days in the house was getting through and convincing the others I was a celebrity. But there were lots of other things happening around me, most of which I tried my best to keep out of.

There had been huge rows about Pete's 'gorilla' coat. There was an increasing dislike of Jodie from the older housemates, which I couldn't understand. I didn't hear her talking crudely about sex, though I now know from the videos that she did. The thing about *Big Brother* is that the hour-long highlights programme the viewers see every day is heavily edited. But they can never make things up: they can only show things that people did and said in there. So Jodie definitely gave them the ammunition.

I don't like hearing girls – or blokes – talk crudely about sex. It's horrible. But I didn't know what she had said, and I thought it was very unfair of the others to be ganging up against her. George had a real go at her on the day of the fame test, and I was amazed at his attitude.

The thing about Jodie is that she would be brilliant on a normal *Big Brother*, where the house is full of young people, running around and being mental together. Perhaps that's what she was expecting. Then her attitudes, and the things she said, would not have seemed out of place.

From the very beginning, I thought George was a sneaky, crafty sort of person. Later on, I changed my mind and liked him – but in the end I decided that my first instincts about him were right.

One thing I do remember from that day was Dennis trying to proposition me, again, in his usual unsubtle way.

'Before you leave the house, we'll have sex, OK?' he said.

I laughed and asked if he was telling me or asking me. It went completely over my head. I didn't find him scary, but I knew one day he would turn on me and have a go at me: I saw him do it to some of the others, and I knew my turn would come. I was determined never to let him reduce me to tears, and I prepared myself for it.

Later that day all the girls compared notes about how he was propositioning them.

I said: 'No way, José,' and everyone agreed with me.

There are two little things I will never forget from that weird and surreal day:

One was Faria telling us how she once peed into the cup of tea of a boyfriend she didn't like, and then enjoyed watching him drink it. That's one of the most gross things I've ever heard!

And the other was Rula sticking her finger into my champagne glass to stop it fizzing over. Imagine sticking your dirty finger into someone else's glass – you are meant to do it with a spoon handle. Ever since then, whenever Preston and I open champagne, we joke about Rula sticking her finger in my glass.

Chapter Nine

Tears and Tantrums

I was walking on air the next day. If I had a hangover – and I think I should have done – I was too happy to notice it. I was just so thrilled to have made it. I didn't think about how far I would get – if I'd been evicted the next day, I would still have felt like a winner. I certainly didn't give a thought to how long the show would be running and how many days I might be in there. I know Davina wound up the live show the night before by saying: 'Chantelle has left us with the possibility that a non-celebrity could win *Celebrity Big Brother*.' But it honestly wasn't a thought that crossed my mind.

We had to make our first nominations that day, and I always had to go first, because it was in alphabetical order. Nominations are a terrible thing, as anyone who has been on *Big Brother* will tell you. You have to choose two people, whether you want to or not.

I chose Rula, because I felt she was rude and controlling, and she didn't like me. I also chose George.

I said: 'He always thinks he is right. What he says is like an order in court, but we're not in the Houses of Parliament now. I can imagine he feels I'm a stupid young girl.'

I didn't get any nominations at all – I honestly expected I would, because I thought some people would feel I was there under false pretences. Jodie got by far the most, with seven, and George and Pete both got four.

Preston teased me that he had nominated me for being 'a lying bitch', but I knew he hadn't. He and Pete really made me laugh by talking about how fame would go to my head. Pete said I'd be 'a right diva in two weeks. She'll be changing her clothes every hour, always looking in the mirror. I thought she'd wake up this morning wearing big Chanel sunglasses, a headscarf, a fur coat and saying, "OK, darling, bring me my coffee." '

I could never take Pete seriously. Just looking at him made me laugh. While we were in there we played the game of trying to stare each other out. He always won. I collapsed giggling every time.

There were a lot of complaints from the other housemates about the length of time Pete spent in the shower. I couldn't understand what they were moaning about, because he always waited until everyone else had had their showers. We had two separate toilets, so there was no problem. Pete had to spend extra time in there dressing a wound in his stomach, where he had had flesh removed to put into his lips. He took me into the toilet once to show me the wound: I think he just wanted someone to understand what he had to do.

We weren't told the results of the nominations until the next day. George and Pete acted as if they didn't care, but Jodie cried. I felt really bad for her, although I wouldn't have been so upset if it was me. After all, it's only a game.

It was a helluva day, though. We had to do a task to earn our shopping money, but that was a small sideshow compared to what kicked off in the house later, and I was unwittingly at the centre of it all.

I was really, really tired. I hadn't recovered from the long night of my party. You don't get chance to have a proper lie-in, because the lights come on and there's a blast of noise to wake you up. Also, I think I had been under so much pressure for the first four days, I simply hadn't relaxed. It was all catching up with me, and I'd reached that stage of exhaustion where I could hardly put one foot in front of the other.

Jodie and I took duvets and went over to the settees to sleep, while the rest of them were hanging out together, talking. We didn't deliberately separate ourselves. Jodie was my friend, we talked about hair and make-up and clothes, all the things I'm interested in. But behind our backs some of the others read something sinister and deliberate into our friendship.

I knew nothing about it until all hell broke loose around me. But I now know that Pete was one of the instigators.

He said: 'I am outraged to see Chantelle being educated over there and dragged into a separate camp and becoming as miserable as the sour old cow herself, and probably coerced into topless modelling because it makes loads of money . . .'

Looking back, it's funny that he should make such a big deal about me doing topless modelling (he said a lot more about it in the days to come) when in fact I'd already done it – and was proud of it! I hadn't made any secret of it in the house – I'd told people that I'd done Page Three-type pictures, but nobody seemed to believe it or take any notice of it. Anyway, I don't think the topless modelling stuff had anything to do with what happened next.

Michael came over to us as we tried to sleep to persuade us to go over and join the others. I resented him interfering, what we were doing was nothing to do with him. The rest of the housemates took time out – Dennis and Traci were always off in the gym, but nobody got on their case about not being with the others. Michael was really rude and condescending to me.

'Let me finish, darling, please. If you're going to be a celebrity you've got to adopt a different attitude . . .'

I told him I was a normal person. He accused me of jumping in and interrupting him, and eventually he went away and left us alone. But this was just the beginning of an eventful day – I call it the Night of the Big Rows, Mark One.

The task we were all having to do was to test scientific ideas. Faria had to eat spinach to see if it really did make her strong, Jodie and Traci had to listen to classical music to see if it made them more intelligent.

Preston had to eat fifty chocolate liqueurs in two hours, to see if it put him over the drink-driving limit. It was a horrible task, and he was sick in the toilet three times, trying to stuff them down. Michael was unwrapping them for him, and I was helping him by making sure he had water. When he was near the end I gave him a little cuddle and told him to keep going, that he was doing well – all the usual stuff you say to someone who is near the end of a race, just to cheer them on.

Suddenly Michael went off on one at me. I just don't know what that was all about. He told me off for distracting Preston, when all I was doing was helping him. He said I should give Preston a bit of space, and I should be quiet. Michael seemed to be very manic, and I was a bit scared. Not because I thought he was dangerous, but because I thought he was flipping and getting out of control. I stood up for myself, but later, I now know, he complained that 'the girls talk to me like a piece of shit'.

'Chantelle is being led by the other one. Now I'm getting lip from her. She'll turn into a fucking monster if she allows that. It's not fair, it's not fair on her. It's fucking out of order. It's fucking dangerous.'

George, Rula and Pete joined in.

George said: 'You can't have a child talking to a man of his age in this way. The girl wasn't like it . . .'

Pete said: 'As a group we need to make a statement about this. It makes me sick – that's a child being led astray.'

Looking back at it now, I feel outraged that they talked about me as a child so much. I was twenty-two when I was in the house, quite old enough to look after myself and make my own decisions. I hadn't been led astray – that may have been their opinion, because they thought Jodie had too much influence over me, but I disagree. And by the time the whole three weeks was up, I think I proved that I was one of the few mature people in there. Anyway, if I was a child, surely Michael was out of order in the way he treated 'the child'.

While they were having a go at me, I went into the Diary Room with Jodie – where she proceeded to rip into Michael. Her words were strong, but Michael had been having a real go at her. I now know it was because he heard her talking about him when he was behind the bedroom door, but it would have been better if he had simply confronted her about it. Then, at least, she would have known why he was being horrible to her.

We were in there for a long time, more than twenty minutes, and outside the others were convinced we were being nasty about Michael. When we came out, it was like a bomb going off. George, Dennis and Maggot tried to warn me about getting too close to Jodie. I was like 'Whaaat???' I'd just been loyal to Jodie – it would have been so easy to go with the majority and abandon her, but I couldn't do that.

When Jodie joined us, it really kicked off. They ignored me, and all went for her. George said: 'The facts are that you have turned that young girl, who was a perfect angel a couple of days ago. You are a wicked person. You are causing absolute strife in here, and you have inveigled that young girl.'

They were all so nasty to Jodie that I felt worried for her. But I was also worried when one of them said that Michael was in the garden crying.

'Why is Michael crying? Is it because of him and me?' I asked.

Pete said it was, but added that I'd been led astray.

I felt upset to think I'd caused him to cry, even though I knew he was being ridiculous. I went out into the garden to see him, and we talked. He said it put him in a bad place, having to tell me to back off, and not to talk to him like I had done.

I still felt that I had done nothing wrong, but I comforted him and hugged him. Inside the house, they were still going great guns, laying into Jodie. Later on, when it had calmed down a bit, I told Pete, Michael, Preston and George how I felt. I'm really proud of the little speech I made:

'I like Jodie and I like all of you, but it's hard for me to be with Jodie and with the rest of you, because the rest of you are feeling this hostility towards Jodie. I find it hard to be having a conversation with Jodie. Jodie can't join in jokes with you. I'm piggy in the middle. I know this is a big thing for you, but can you imagine how it is for me?'

Preston, who is always the sensible one, suggested everyone should work at making better relationships, but Pete quickly said he didn't want a better relationship with Jodie. Jodie went off to bed early, and I stayed up chatting with the others. I sat next to Preston, mainly because I felt he had not been getting at me, and he was my friend.

I didn't get a good sleep that night – but not because of all the rows. Maggot and I had to sleep in the 'science lab' with a tape of the Japanese language being played all night, to see if we could learn it in our sleep. It was very hot in there, and I can never sleep with the sound of a radio or television.

The next morning, Maggot wound me up by pretending he was now fluent in Japanese – very funny. I always liked Maggot, from the very beginning. If he had something to say, he tried to do it in a nice way. I know that later on he tried to vote me off, but that's the game, you have to nominate somebody, and I really don't mind at all.

When we went into the Diary Room to be questioned in Japanese, we were, of course, hopeless. If only we had known we were being asked if we would like champagne and chocolate cake!

Pete and Dennis were given an easy task: they had to look after a plant each, and talk to it to see if that made it grow. Pete didn't make much of an effort, which he may have thought was funny. But we knew that if we failed the task, we'd have a shopping budget of only £1 per day each. I wasn't too worried, as I don't smoke and I'm happy not to drink. But Pete's a smoker, so you would have thought he would have taken it all a bit more seriously.

Rula and George had to act out some animal experiments, and this was when the most infamous clip from the whole series happened. George, a Member of Parliament, was filmed play-acting at being a cat. He was seen sipping cream from Rula's hands. I had absolutely no idea that this was going on – and even if I had seen them, I probably wouldn't have thought anything of it. I know it caused an uproar outside the house, but inside, it was nothing.

When we got the task results, I was convinced we had

managed to do it. But we'd failed. George said he was glad: he looked forward to the test of having to live on a £1 a day.

Pete said one of his very funny things: 'Let's just kill Dennis. We could live on him for three weeks.'

Jodie was still an outsider, and very unhappy. I couldn't see any solution, because the others seemed determined not to give her another chance. When she was talking to Big Brother in the Diary Room, she said there were only three people in the house who hadn't attacked her: me, Preston and Faria. But she added that I could have helped her more, by telling everybody that I had invited her to go with me into the Diary Room (the time the others thought we were slagging off Michael in there).

'Chantelle could make everyone like me again,' she said, 'and realise that I am not a bad person.'

I think this was a very unfair comment, after all the loyalty I'd shown her. I can't remember ever asking her to go with me in the Diary Room. And how could I have made them like her?

Even though I didn't, of course, know that Jodie was being critical of me, I still felt a very heavy atmosphere hanging over the house. We'd lost our shopping money, which didn't bother me too much, but we'd also had the whole series of anti-Jodie rows. Add on the fact that I was very, very tired, having had so little sleep in the science lab.

After our evening meal I sat quietly with Preston. We talked about our lives outside the house, and it hit me in a great wave how much I missed my mum, and I told him.

He was really sweet. I can't remember everything he said, but I know he put his arm around me, and he told me I was 'gorgeous'. We were getting on so well, but I didn't think any more of it. He made me feel good, and I liked being with him. Even at this stage, I think we were both suppressing our feelings for each other, because when I look at the video I can see that we looked at each other very lovingly.

The next day we had what I call the Quorn War. It was just another excuse for everyone to have a go at Jodie. Michael was the main culprit, and it all got out of hand. It sounds so petty now, out here, when we can all just open the fridge or a cupboard, or pop down to the shops to get something to eat. But in there, food is very important, especially when there is so little money to buy it.

Me, Traci and Jodie were vegetarians, and on every shopping order we'd ask for some Quorn, a vegetable protein used as a meat substitute. Michael did almost all the cooking in there. (He did most of the cleaning, too, but it was not because the rest of us were lazy. He seemed to like to keep himself busy.) He was a brilliant cook, which we really appreciated during the time we were living with so little money. He could make a great meal out of anything.

Anyway, sometimes he would make a big meal using Quorn, which everyone would eat. Then the Quorn would run out and the only protein left would be meat, which me, Traci and Jodie didn't eat. (Remember I don't eat cheese, either.)

Anyway, a big row blew up about the Quorn, with Michael really shouting at Jodie. I was trying to calm them both down, but not very successfully. Michael kept telling me that he wasn't angry with me, but he was having a real rant at Jodie. I felt very sorry for her and very worried for him. I felt he was losing it again.

In the end, I somehow persuaded them to stop rowing and hug each other, although from their body language it was plain that neither of them really felt better.

I was wearing long stripy socks, a short yellow skirt and a black top – Pete said I looked like a buzzy little bee. I had enough clothes with me in there to last me the whole three weeks without having to wash any. I think I only doubled up by wearing my tracksuits more than once.

The others washed out their underwear in the kitchen sink, but there was never any mess of wet washing around the house, as they dried it in the sauna. I never used the sauna, although I did pop in there now and again just to warm up. It was January, and very cold outside, and not always warm enough in the house. But I wouldn't use it as a sauna because I was worried that it would bring out spots. I never used the gym, either – even though it was decorated in my favourite colour. I've only recently started going to a gym, to tone myself up. I've never been that keen on exercise.

Finally, on our ninth day in the house, it was time for the first eviction. There was an extra tension in the air all day. Jodie told us that she was desperate to go, and I think by this time she meant it. She really wasn't having a nice experience in there. But I was desperately hoping it would be George who would be booted out. I thought that without him, Jodie might be able to make friends with some of the others.

She told me and Preston her plans if she went out:

'I could go out tonight, get wrecked, snog a fit bloke, stick my tongue down his throat for fun, have someone to hold my hair while I'm being sick, and then go to bed with my dogs.'

I don't think that endeared her to any of the other housemates who heard it. George said about the only witty thing I heard him say the whole time he was there. After Jodie called him immoral, he said:

'Being called immoral by Jodie is a bit like being told to sit up straight by the Hunchback of Notre-Dame.'

It was Friday the 13th, and it was also Traci's birthday. Big Brother set her a task which, if she did it, would mean we could all have a party. She had to retrieve plastic skulls from a 'swamp' – a trough full of horrible goo. I was so glad I didn't have to immerse my hair in it. Traci was very good about doing it, and she won us our party. But before we could celebrate, we had the horrible business of the eviction to go through.

I was glad when Jodie's name was called, for her sake. But, for my sake, I really didn't want her to go. When I watch the videos of the programme, all I see are the bits where Jodie was rowing with people. The fun we had together wasn't shown. We were always larking about, singing, dancing, playing about in the pool.

When she left, you can see from video how deflated and quiet I was. I felt I'd made a friend, and then she'd gone. I cried a bit, and Preston gave me a long hug. Although he liked Jodie, he said something very wise:

'We all get along in here now. Much as I love Jodie, now there's no friction.'

When she left, Jodie told Davina that her time in the house had been 'hideous, evil'. But she said lovely things about me, and she told the audience to all vote for me to win. Later on she phoned my mum, which was really nice of her.

It was a good night to have a party: we needed something to lift our spirits. We all had freaky Friday the 13th costumes. I think mine was meant to be the Bride of Dracula. It was very low cut, and it was only at the end of the evening that me and Preston realised I had it on the wrong way round – it was meant to be low at the back.

We had lots to eat and drink, but by the end of the evening I was feeling a bit tearful again. I was sitting with Preston, and I told him I was a bit drunk. He put his arm round me and rubbed my back. This is what we said:

Preston: 'Don't be upset, you'll see her again.'

Me: 'It was on top of missing my mum. I'm not really a baby, am I?'

Preston: 'You're a total little baby . . .'

Me: 'I think I need to go to bed.'

Preston: 'If you get upset, just come and see me. I can treat you like I treat my sister.'

It was a really sweet little chat, and I was so grateful to him for being so nice to me when I was feeling low. I knew I was liking him more and more. But it was very early days in our romance, and I didn't read anything into it. I just felt flattered that he liked me enough to fool around with me like that.

By the time I'd got into bed I'd cheered up a bit. I was telling the others, most of whom were in bed, what my plans were for when I got out of the house.

'I'm going to get my nails done again, and have a sunbed. And I want to get married, as well.'

I was only fooling around, because I'd never wanted to get married.

Traci said: 'Who to?'

I said: 'I don't know yet.'

Preston said: 'Chantelle, if I didn't have a girlfriend, I'd marry you in a minute.'

I said, 'I'd marry you, too.' I felt all warm inside, but I just thought he was letting me know that he liked me. It was lovely to know that he thought I was a nice person. Looking back, I can see I had begun to fancy him, but at the time I simply did not allow myself to think of him in that way, because he wasn't available. I'd known from the very beginning that he had a girlfriend – I can't remember when I found out, but it was in those first couple of days, before I was close to him. So it felt as though I had always known it, and it meant that he was off-limits.

The rest of them all started to coo and congratulate us.

Pete said: 'You'd be like a little scally couple.'

And Traci added: 'So sweet.'

I must have been drunk because I started singing 'I'm getting married in the morning' and Preston then sang 'Going to the chapel and we're gonna get married'.

It was just a bit of fun. But it's so weird to look back at it now. We had no idea that one day our little bit of fun would turn into a reality . . .

Chapter Ten

An Ordinary Boy

There's a strange thing about the *Big Brother* house. When someone leaves, of course you miss them. But in hardly any time at all, the rest of the housemates re-form and it's as if the ones who have gone have never even been there. Of course I missed Jodie, but not as much as I thought I would.

The first thing we did the next day was the box task, where we had to lie inside cardboard boxes. We walked into the room full of boxes, each labelled with our names.

Pete said: 'It looks like a Yoko Ono exhibition.'

The idea was to see who could stay there the longest. It may sound odd, but I really loved being inside my box. It was peaceful, nobody could see me. I could be on my own without anyone thinking I was sitting in a corner isolating myself from the others. I didn't have to worry about the expression on my face, as there was nobody to see it and accuse me of being miserable. Not that I was miserable, but in the house everyone is so acutely aware of each other that if you have a straight face for ten minutes, the others start worrying about you.

It was good to have time to myself, to think over the last few days. So I would have stayed in there, but George took over and told us all to come out. After a few minutes I couldn't be bothered with all the grief and arguing, so I came out.

When Sir Jimmy Savile came in, I genuinely didn't know who he was. I thought he was Bruce Forsyth. George had to whisper in my ear. I didn't recognise the *Jim'll Fix It* music, but I'd heard the expression 'Jim'll Fix It'. I was astonished by how much gold he was wearing. We all had to ask him to fix something for us, and I couldn't think what, so I wrote down 'Please make me a pop star'.

It was good sitting around listening to Jimmy Savile. He seemed to know everybody in show business, and he had lots of stories which made a bit of a change for us all.

After so many days with only each other for company, I suppose it was natural that we began to grate on each other a bit. I know from watching the video that Pete was fed up with me, although I didn't pick up on it.

'I'm getting irritable. The little things are starting to annoy me,' he told Big Brother in the Diary Room. 'The sound of Chantelle's voice, though she's adorable. I'm really finding her Doris Dimbleby act really irritating . . . She has started to play on my nerves. OK, you got what you came for, you won the pop star thing. Come on, you are in your twenties, you can't possibly be that dumb. Stupidity has a charm, but after a while it starts to grate. She's so naive, it's starting to get to me.'

I think that's funny. If he'd said it to my face, I'd have laughed. I was never offended by Pete, although I know that towards the end he did get very bitchy. But I still could never take him seriously. I just had to look at him and I started giggling.

There was a really funny moment that evening, when Preston, Maggot and me were sitting around.

Preston said: '*OK!* magazine will want exclusive pictures of our wedding.'

I said: 'Completely. When are you going to give me my ring?'

Maggot added: 'They'll offer you thousands and thousands of pounds.'

Then Preston took his signet ring off and put it on my finger. I went round the house showing everyone, and Faria gave me a big hug. It was just a great laugh, and I gave him back the ring straight away. But look how true it turned out to be!

We were really enjoying each other's company. He was my best friend, and we spent as much time as possible together. Not because we didn't get on with the others, but we felt comfortable together, and we made each other laugh. With Maggot, we were the young ones, so it was natural we formed a little group. We talked about our lives, and I obviously knew he was with a girl, and he knew about my previous boyfriends. Giving me the signet ring had been a joke, and I didn't think anything about it. I guess we were just flirting, but it was harmless and innocent.

I've now seen on video what Preston said about me in the Diary Room, and it's so nice to hear. I felt completely the same about him.

'Chantelle is, like, she's fucking wicked. She's a constant source of hilarity, isn't she? I find I get on really, really well with her. The worst thing would be if I was to last a long time and she was to go. I can't see that happening. If she left, maybe it would change. While she's here, if anything gets too heavy and people are arguing, I can do something silly with Chantelle and laugh.

'I laughed so much yesterday I was almost sick, my stomach was hurting – and nothing really funny happened, either. She's a lot cleverer than anyone thinks. She's streetwise. She may not have the same general knowledge as George or Rula, but she knows human nature more than people give her credit for. I really, really like her.'

Me and Preston didn't think anything about being so close. It just came naturally, and it never occurred to us that the other housemates – and the world outside – might think we were falling in love. Looking back, we *were* falling in love, but we certainly never admitted it to ourselves, even in our most private moments. As far as I was concerned – and I know Preston felt the same – it was a great friendship. It is very, very boring in the house, which you have no idea about if you watch the nightly television programmes. In one hour they show you the day's highlights, but there is so much time spent just sitting around with absolutely nothing to do. So if you find a soulmate to pass the time with, have some laughs and make the day go faster, you don't read anything more into it.

But one time, when Preston was exercising and he asked me to pull his arms, Pete alerted us to what people might be saying on the outside and that the press would have a field day.

Then Pete went off on a riff about me. It was very Pete, very funny, and it would have been offensive if anyone else had said it.

'The sad thing is, as you grow older, your brain cells actually diminish, so you're in real trouble. You're at your sharpest now, love. Next time you get your teeth flossed, see if he can do your brain as well, plaque removal.'

I didn't feel insulted, I just giggled all the way through.

We didn't know it, but with his comments about how the outside world might be seeing us, Pete was just expressing what the other housemates were saying to each other. Michael and Faria had a conversation about it, too.

Preston went into the Diary Room.

'I want to clear something up,' he said. 'Everybody, especially Pete, is implying that me and Chantelle are having some secret affair or something. It ain't like that at all. We haven't done anything wrong. Just because she's young and I'm young, so we're silly together. Now that's been said I feel I won't be able to be relaxed around her. I want to clear it up. I think she's tops, I really like her, I think she's wicked. But not like that.'

I didn't think the others had any right to be making

comments about us. It was unfair. They made much more of it than it was. Preston and I did spend a lot of time together, but we also spent lots of time with the others. Maggot was often fooling around with us.

I talked to Faria about it.

'Every boyfriend I've ever had has cheated on me. However much I liked someone I wouldn't dream of kissing them or anything. Even if there was something between me and Preston, I wouldn't dream of kissing him because of the fact that he's got a girlfriend, even if Preston was saying it doesn't matter. I wouldn't like it done to me.'

That was how I felt then, and it is how I feel today. I would never, knowingly, split someone from their girlfriend.

After that I made a big effort to stay away from him, walking past him without even looking at him. But that was very hard to do, especially in a confined space like the house. Outside, if you want to stay away from someone, it's very easy. In there, it becomes a big thing if you try to avoid each other.

Me and Preston had a chance to talk about it later. I said I hoped he wasn't worried about it.

'I'm not worried at all, Chantelle,' he said. 'Only in a silly way. To me it's just funny. It's stupid. If we get on really well, like we do, who cares what people think. It's more important that we stay sane in here. Us two just laugh about it when the others find it tough.'

I told him I was only thinking of him.

He said: 'If you want to think of me, don't do anything different. I think you're wicked.'

I said: 'I think you're wicked too. Oh God . . .'

Later on, Preston talked to George and Maggot about it. He said he thought Big Brother wanted me and him to get drunk and fall into each other's arms. George told him not to beat himself up about it, and Maggot told him to enjoy it, but remember . . . I think he meant remember the cameras, although I think at the time Preston was more worried about Pete, who seemed to be making such a thing about our relationship.

Late at night Preston and me talked again.

He said: 'If people think we're having some secret relationship I will take that risk in order for you and me to get on. My priority is for you and me to get along.'

He moved to sit next to me, and we were giggling about something and I instinctively just put my head on his shoulder. He put his arm round me and kissed the side of my head. Then his arm slipped to round my waist. I'm sure I was aware of it a bit at the time, but it all seemed so natural. Of course, the others were taking note: even Dennis and Traci, who were the least observant of the housemates, were now talking about us.

We had a very tender little conversation, but you have to remember that it was in the context of Michael sitting with us. We weren't going away in private just to be together.

Preston said: 'With you, I've got a temporary replacement for the people I love outside.'

Me: 'Not an added extra, just a replacement?'

Preston: 'Yeah, just a temporary replacement, like a disposable camera.'

Me: 'Oh my God!'

Michael intervened, and told Preston that wasn't the smoothest thing to say.

'You've delivered better sentences. I would rewind that one.'

Preston gave me a hug and then said: 'You have the qualities that are unique to the people I love. You are the type of person that I love.'

We had another hug and Preston added: 'That's what keeps me sane. That's why I haven't been emotional – because you were here.'

I just said, 'Ditto,' and then Preston winked at me.

Writing it down for this book, and watching it again on the video, it's obvious to me as well as to everyone else that we were falling in love. But I really was in denial: I never admitted to myself what was happening. I thought the others were just making an issue of it because they didn't like the fact that Preston and me had a really close friendship, which was helping us get through.

But of course, something much deeper was happening. I was denying to myself my own feelings for him. But there were clues that I could have picked up on. At about this time I really became aware of putting my make-up on before he saw me in the morning: I didn't want him to see me without it, even though he'd seen me like that plenty of times in the early days in the house. And one morning I remember waking up, then checking that he was still in bed, and going back to sleep. I didn't want to get up if he wasn't around.

I'd never met a man like him.

*

It was Preston's twenty-fourth birthday, and I so wanted to do something for him. I went into the toilet and made a card for him, using my eyeliner pencil and a piece of card left over from one of the tasks. But then I thought about what everyone would say, and how it would fuel all the speculation about us, so I threw it away.

It was a nominations day, which isn't nice on your birthday. It was horrible, but I didn't have any trouble deciding who I was going to choose: Dennis and George. I selected Dennis because he was always watching me, and it made me feel uncomfortable. My reasons for George were much the same as they had been the previous time:

'He's got some sort of military style of talking to younger people. I respected him until he started screaming and getting angry. He thinks he's in charge.'

I got two nominations, and I really didn't resent them. We all had to do it, and we all had to choose someone. Dennis's reasons for choosing me were a bit two-faced. He tried to make himself look nice by suggesting he was doing me a favour.

'Chantelle's kinda lost in here. She's just overwhelmed by what's going on. She misses her mother, which I can understand. She needs to find a way, and this is not it.'

Like I say, I didn't mind being nominated, but it's bullshit to pretend he was doing it for my sake. Pete also nominated me.

Preston nominated Traci and Dennis, mainly because the two of them did seem to be living a separate life from the rest of us, always in the gym together or just talking together.

Explaining his nomination, Pretson said: 'Me and Chantelle were getting on really well last night, having a lovely time, a little cuddle and everything. I hadn't thought about how it would look and he's been going on about it all day. It's doing my head in.'

That night we had a birthday party for Preston, a mods and rockers party. I had a long pencil skirt, a roll-neck sweater and a trench coat. I would never have chosen clothes like that, but once I'd put it all on I quite liked the look. Preston looked really cool in his sharp mod suit – that style looks good on him.

We had a great lark. Music, alcohol, food – it was a real treat, as we were living on £1 a day food rations. Not that we were ever hungry, as Michael was so inventive in the kitchen. And we were very lucky that both Traci's party and Preston's party meant extra supplies.

At the end of the day, after I'd gone to bed Preston told a group of the others:

'I've laughed more in the last two weeks than in the rest of my life.'

I have to agree with that: the *Big Brother* house to me was just one big laugh. I know some people get stressed out by it, but I think they take it too seriously, and lose sight of the fact that it is only light-hearted fun.

The next day, Day 13, we were given the nomination results. Rula had been allowed to make her own guaranteed nomination, as her extra special prize for winning the cardboard box game. She chose Pete. Dennis and Faria were both up because of our nominations. I was relieved my name wasn't on the list, but I never felt as tense about nominations as some of the others did. Every day was a bonus for me: I never imagined I would last this long, and I still couldn't believe what was happening. As I've said before, if I'd gone out after four days I would have felt like a winner.

Poor old Traci had a terrible experience that morning. She was lying in bed when George and Rula came into the bedroom, and Rula started bitching about her not realising she was there. If it had been me, I think I would have said something to Rula, but Traci didn't, she just got up from her bed and walked out of the room. I think she confided in Faria.

There was a huge row about racism that morning – Dennis was going mad. It was mental, and I just kept completely out of the way. Big Brother then told us we had to choose a housemate who was calm and articulate under pressure, although we didn't know why at the time. George was unanimously chosen, and it turned out that he was on the *Richard & Judy* programme playing 'You Say, We Pay'. Instead of winning the usual thousands of pounds, he won £140 for our shopping budget, which was really great. I was looking forward to having some Quorn again, and nice bread instead of the cheap stuff we had to buy on our £1 a day budget.

We were woken on eviction day to the sound of bells tolling – not a very cheerful start to the day. I was chatting with Maggot when he said he came from South Wales, and I said something silly which in the end had a great significance.

I said: 'Do you live anywhere near Dundee?'

I don't know why I though Dundee was in Wales, but I was never any good at that sort of thing. It was funny, me being so ignorant, and I did think: 'I bet they show that clip on TV.' I realised it made me look like a real dumb blonde.

Eviction days are always long and difficult, but the afternoon was cheered up by Big Brother asking us all to do self-portraits. I can't paint, but I loved having something to do. I did a very colourful picture, with red cheeks and lips, blue eyes and blue earrings, and very blonde hair. Then we had to explain them.

I said: 'This is me cos I'm bright – not bright as in clever bright, but bright as in colourful bright. I like bright make-up, I love earrings, the whole bright thing. I'm smiling because I'm happy. That's me: bright, bright, bright.'

When the eviction announcement came, it was Faria. I was surprised, as I felt it would probably be Dennis. I never felt I got to know Faria very well, and I don't think she got close to anybody, really. If she had a fault, it's that she tried too hard to be nice when she should have relaxed because she is nice anyway. She went out to a mixture of boos and cheers, and when I watched the video of her interview, I felt really moved that she told everyone to vote for me as I should win because 'she so deserves it'. Thank you, Faria, that was lovely of you.

After she'd gone, there was the usual feeling of anticlimax that there always is after an eviction. Following on from me not knowing that Dundee was in Scotland, Maggot started to test me on places. He asked me the capital of Scotland, which I got straight away. Then he asked me the capital of France. I was a bit flustered and I said Brussels or Belgium before I corrected myself and said Paris. I didn't think Maggot was having a go at me, and as I don't care that I don't know those sort of things it really didn't bother me. If I had been the sort of person who felt they ought to know, maybe I would have been upset, but I didn't take offence.

Preston did, though. He was upset, because he thought Maggot was deliberately trying to make me look foolish. He went into the bedroom and told Pete what was happening.

Pete said: 'What's she supposed to be? A geography teacher? She's smart enough to win. She's amazing, a ray of sunshine. She never gets down, ever.'

Preston agreed. 'I love that, she's wicked.'

(I don't think anybody who watched the show was surprised by Pete's turnaround – that's just the way he is.)

Of course, I knew nothing about this, and I didn't even realise that Preston was upset with Maggot. But I'm very, very touched that he cared about me like that.

The next thing that happened was one of the worst incidents in my time in the house, and for once I really did feel miserable about it. We were all sitting around the dining-room table, when George and Preston were called to the Diary Room together. Outside, we were gobsmacked when the screen came on and we realised we could see them in there – and hear them. They had no idea we could.

Big Brother told them that they had broken the rules by discussing nominations, and that as a punishment they must nominate three housemates to face the public vote. It was horrible seeing Preston in that situation. Nominations are bad enough normally, but this was terrible. I really felt for him.

Later, when I had time to think about it, I realised it was very unfair. George had been in trouble before for discussing nominations, so had Dennis and Traci. Preston had done it just once, and had confessed afterwards and apologised in the Diary Room, and yet he was getting this massive punishment.

They had to make their minds up quickly, and they both agreed on Traci. Outside, listening to them, Traci was going mental. Then Preston suggested Maggot.

'He said "let's play the capital cities game". To me it was "let's make Chantelle look like a wanker game".'

I felt so pleased that he was standing up for me, even though I hadn't been bothered about the game. George agreed with his nomination, and then they decided on Rula as the third. George said he thought she was trying too hard and was now saying she would win.

When they came out of the Diary Room, at first some of the others pretended not to know what had happened. But I went to Preston and gave him a hug, and told him he was such a nice bloke. I wanted him to know that I was on his side. I knew there would be lots of arguments kicking off about what had happened, and I wanted him to know I would be there for him.

There were, of course, lots of repercussions, especially as everyone had had quite a lot to drink now that we had lots of shopping money. Maggot apologised to me, and I accepted his apology willingly, as I never thought he meant anything nasty. Then Preston apologised to Maggot, but Maggot was obviously a bit hurt.

'If you thought I was trying to make her look an idiot you should have said,' he told Preston.

Rula was understanding, remembering how she had had to nominate someone, and Maggot told George not to worry. Preston and George both agreed that they regretted nominating Maggot. It seemed to be going well, everyone was being remarkably civilised.

But then friction broke out between Maggot and George. Maggot accused George of saying I was 'as daft as a brush'. George admitted he had, but insisted it was different to Maggot teasing me about the capital cities. Maggot accused him of being a backstabber, I just wished they'd both shut up: I really wasn't bothered about the things they had said. But I must say, given a choice, I'd rather have Maggot teasing me to my face than George saying things behind my back. I reckon that Maggot was completely right when he called George a backstabber. I'd seen him doing it to other people, and I'd never had any illusions about him.

There was more to come: Pete went off on a wild riff slagging off Traci.

I didn't have to be Mystic Meg to predict that there would be trouble before we went to bed. But I certainly didn't know that once we got to bed, the trouble would carry on . . . and on . . . and on . . .

Chapter Eleven

Rows, Rows and More Rows

What a night! After Jodie had left the house, I'd moved into her bed to be away from Dennis's snoring. This meant I was sleeping next to Traci, which wasn't normally a problem. But getting nominated got to her, and she became a neurotic mess. She didn't sleep all night, which meant I didn't either. At ten to five in the morning the whole room was awake, listening to her going on about it. It really did my head in: it was difficult getting enough sleep in there without having to put up with this.

At first I tried to be nice, telling her it would all seem better in the morning, and not to worry. I told her everyone had to go some time, and reminded her that it was only a game show, after all. Like I said to her, it wasn't like being chucked out of your house in real life. And I told her that we'd all been drinking, and that made things seem worse.

But in the end, I got fed up trying to persuade her to stop

complaining and worrying and go to sleep. In the end I snapped at her, telling her to 'shut up'.

Needless to say, nobody was very pleased with her the next day. Pete did a wicked impression of her, and Preston said he was ten times more upset about nominating Maggot and Rula than he was about Traci.

Maggot was talking to Big Brother in the Diary Room, and he summed up the feeling in the house that morning well:

'There's a heavy, hung-over feeling in the house. People are not sure what to do, what to say, where to place themselves.'

That's exactly how it felt, as if we were all walking on eggshells, waiting for something to erupt. Which it did, of course.

Maggot went on to tell Big Brother about Preston, and when I saw what he said on the video later I was sorry, because he and Preston and me had really got on well for such a long time. He said he hadn't realised that Preston was so wrapped up in me, and that Preston couldn't make eye contact with him, probably because he was feeling guilty. I know Preston was feeling very bad about Maggot, but at the same time, if he hadn't been nominated it would have been someone else.

Pete was very anti Traci all day, probably because she had completely ruined his – and everyone else's – beauty sleep.

He said about her: 'Scratch the surface and what do you find? More surface.'

But he said something very, very nice to me. (I think Pete

found it hard to let his niceness out – it was always easier for him to say something witty and cruel.)

He said: 'I've got a whole new respect for you after the last two days, the way you've said "Hey, enough!" You've been one of the least freaked out. I've totally fucking fallen for you. I think you're fucking great.'

We had a hug. I wasn't the only one who coped well with the pressures of being in the house, but I think in my case it was easier because I had no expectations from being there. I didn't have a career I needed to revive. For me, just being there was the most incredible achievement, and every day I stayed there was a bonus. Some of the others found life in there hard, but I never did. I had times of homesickness when I missed Mum and the rest of my family and friends, but I always knew I would see everybody soon. I genuinely found it great fun being there.

It was a very subdued day, probably because we were all so tired after a disturbed night. People tended to sit around talking quietly, and dozing, for much of the day.

But in the quietness, the seeds of a huge problem were being planted. Rula had taken her nomination well, in the spirit of the game, but obviously she had been shocked to find herself chosen so publicly by George, who had been her great ally and friend.

Trying to justify his choice, George told her that if it had been up to him he would have chosen Preston and me, but obviously he couldn't because Preston was with him – and Preston would never have agreed to me.

I would hate to think that all politicians are like George. He is the only one I have ever met, and I was shocked by how immature and selfish he could be. He had chosen Rula, and he should have had the strength of character to stand by his decision. I know that forcing him and Preston to nominate publicly was quite cruel, but once it's done, you can't sneak around trying to get back in favour the way he did.

If this was a quiet day, the next made up for it. Not only was there a pending eviction, which always made the house feel edgy, but there was also a huge commotion about Pete's 'gorilla' coat, which, unbeknown to any of us, was causing lots of fuss outside the house. There had been so many protests about it that the police had asked for it. When he packed his suitcase for a possible eviction, Big Brother had to take it out and hand it over for testing. It turned out not to be gorilla fur, but colobus monkey fur. That's an endangered species, but not as serious as if it had been gorilla.

When Pete realised it had gone, I think all *Big Brother* housemates were an endangered species. He went mental, ranting about wanting it back, and then refusing to join in with the eviction procedure.

I don't know how he got away with it, because not taking part completely broke the rules. But I guess *Big Brother* just liked having Pete around as he was so funny and entertaining. I kept well out of the row about his coat. It isn't right to kill rare animals, but I didn't feel it was my place to preach to anyone else about what they do.

Some days I missed home and the outside world more than others. It's true that the longer you stay in the house the less things outside matter, but you never stop missing the people you love. That day I put on a pink tracksuit and a pink baseball cap that said 'Princess' across the front. Dean bought the cap for me, at Camden Market, and when I put it on I thought: 'He'll see me wearing it, and he'll be pleased. I bet he's going round saying, "I bought her that."'

It was my way of letting him and Mum know that I was missing them so much. They were missing me, too – apparently Mum kissed the TV screen when they did a close-up on me.

'I know you can't hear me, Chantelle,' she said, 'but I'm going to give you a kiss.' And as she said that I flicked my head, just as though I knew.

All the time I was in there, Mum found it very hard to concentrate on anything. She took lots of her holiday from work, and she admits that on the days she did go in to the office, she wasn't a lot of use. She said that if the firm she worked for wasn't so relaxed and understanding, she'd probably have been sacked, because it was all she could do to type one letter a day.

She had a real scare one day, when someone at work told her that it was up on the Internet that I'd been thrown out of the house. She rang *Big Brother* straight away – they'd given her numbers to ring. It was a terrible moment for her until they said: 'She's very much still in there.'

She, Dean and Dad were all bothered by newspaper reporters. Dad told them a few nice things about me. Mum didn't say anything to anybody: she felt that I was in there on my own doing it, and she didn't want to take any glory from it. None of them found the press intrusive – they were just thrilled that the whole country wanted to know about me. Mum says, looking back, she can't work out how they survived for three weeks, because she was too distracted to do all the normal things like going to the supermarket and cooking meals.

Pete's black mood was broken when he and Preston had a really silly water fight, tearing around the house. Pete sprayed some of that handwash liquid soap all over Preston's hair. I had to laugh, because Pete had told us he could only walk in high heels, as it was impossible to put his feet flat. He said the tendons behind his knee had shortened. But he seemed to be able to run around with Preston in his bare feet.

I had never liked Dennis, but as the days went on I found him more and more unpleasant. He was so rude. I never once heard him say 'please' or 'thank you', and if we were sitting round the table eating he would simply hold out his plate to be given what he wanted, without saying a word. He was definitely the person who got to me more than any other in there at this stage of the game.

Michael was always up before everybody else: he told us he never slept for more than two hours at a time. The others began to notice that he might have an obsessive compulsive disorder because he liked to line everything up straight. He was still doing the cooking and most of the cleaning, but it was his choice. The kitchen became his territory. One day when Preston and me tried to cook the meal he hovered around us, telling us what to do, so in the end we just let him get on with it. He was very good at it, and I think he needed to keep himself busy, so I don't think he felt we were all putting on him or taking him for granted.

When the announcement of the eviction results came, it was Rula who had to go. I was really pleased it wasn't Maggot, but I didn't mind if it was Rula or Traci, as I didn't have a close friendship with either of them. Rula could be controlling: I remember her telling Traci to cover up when she wore a short skirt. It was nothing to do with Rula. I'd never heard of her before I went in there, nor of her famous ex-husband Dennis Waterman – they were both a bit before my time. The fact that she was older didn't matter at all to me. But she could be difficult, and it was a bit of a relief when she'd gone. I don't think she enjoyed the whole experience.

When Davina interviewed her she said that there was nothing going on between me and Preston.

'They are two people of the same age who look cute together. They like each other, but any attraction they may feel for each other is stifled by the consequences of what would happen outside the house.'

She was right that we were now very aware of the consequences of seeming to be too attached to each other. Late that evening Preston sat with me and accused me of ignoring him during the day.

I said: 'I'm doing it for your benefit. I wasn't ignoring you . . . I was just keeping my distance. I was doing it for you, not for any other reason.'

I was really concerned at this stage that people inside and outside the house were speculating that there was something going on between us, and I wanted to avoid causing problems for him when he got out. I remember walking out of the bedroom and straight past Preston, who was sitting at the dining-room table. I tried not to look at him and to keep a straight face, but as soon as I got past I dissolved in giggles.

Earlier that day I had gone to sit by the swimming pool on my own: there were times when I wanted to sit quietly. But then I thought it might look as if I was waiting for him. The longer I sat out there the more ridiculous it seemed. I didn't know whether to stay or go. In the end, I just got up and walked back inside.

We'd now been in the house for two and a half weeks, and nothing could dent my happiness, not even the rows that were going on. I still woke up every morning and almost had to pinch myself to realise where I was, and that I had survived this far. Every day was a bonus, as far as I was concerned, and I still never thought there was the slightest chance of winning. I honestly didn't think about the end of the show: I was taking each day as it came.

So, on the whole, the quarrels and bad moods didn't affect me. But on Day 17 there was a row that really got to me, because it affected Preston – and it showed George in his true colours.

Preston was called to the Diary Room and given an envelope with a card to read out to the rest of the house-mates. He was standing behind the settee, leaning on it, as he read it out, and as he was speaking the words I could see the colour drain from his face. It came as a real shock to him. The message told us all what George had said to Rula about only nominating her because he couldn't nominate Preston and me.

Preston was very hurt, not because he was nearly nominated, but because George was so sneaky, going behind his back and saying things like that. He had a lot of respect for George. I had started out feeling very suspicious of George – I summed him up as crafty and sneaky – then gradually I had changed my views. But now I knew that my gut instinct had been absolutely right. I knew nothing about his political background, but I reckon he must have lost himself a lot of votes by his behaviour in the house.

Typical of a politician, George tried to turn the whole row round on Preston, saying that it was Preston who had maliciously reported him to Big Brother. Preston protested: he'd only reported himself, and it certainly hadn't been malicious. Preston didn't get angry – even to this day I've never seen him angry. He was just totally shocked at what George had said. George accused him of being in a 'terrible strop', which just wasn't true: I think it was George's way of taking the heat off himself. Later on, in the Diary Room, George tried to wriggle out of it and say that he had not said he 'would' have nominated Preston or me, just that he 'could' have. He kept asking Big Brother to check the video.

Well, *I've* checked the video, and he definitely said 'would'. I know it probably all sounds so petty, but I think for Preston it was very important, because he felt his trust had been betrayed. I was really upset for him, without a doubt. For George, it was just another slippery situation that he tried to wriggle out of.

We all had to vote on whether George should be allowed to take part in the next round of nominations. We had a proper polling booth, like in a real election. I'd been in one before when I voted for the first time in the last general election.

When it was Preston's turn to vote he just said: 'A cheating politician, eh? Who'd have thought it?'

Of course, I voted to exclude him from nominating, and so did three of the others. He should have been grateful: nominating was one of the worst things we had to do. But naturally it increased his chances of being up for eviction. It also gave him something to whinge about, as he kept going on about how he had been denied his democratic rights. As if nominating in the *Big Brother* house is that important!

I nominated George and I told Big Brother that I had found him shifty and crafty in the first week 'and I now find this to be completely and utterly true'.

I also nominated Dennis:

'He's disrespectful and rude. He has no manners. He never says "please" or "thank you". They are little words to say, but big words to hear.'

As I left the Diary Room I automatically said, 'Thank you.' Then I popped my head back in and said, 'See, I said "thank you".'

George got the most nominations, but Dennis and me both got three each, so all three of us were up for eviction – although, of course, we weren't told until the next day. I was nominated by Dennis, who said I didn't do much to contribute (like, what were you doing, Dennis?), by Pete and by Traci, who said I was only comfortable around Preston, and also that sometimes she thought I was giving her 'a look'. I don't know what that means, and I was a little bit surprised that she nominated me.

I don't know what I did to Pete, but in the final few days he became quite nasty towards me, not so much to my face as behind my back and in the Diary Room. I'd always been able to laugh Pete's jibes off, because they were so witty, but gradually they became more and more pointed and less funny. Maybe he was a bit bitter that he wasn't a real woman, and I was!

Pete told Big Brother in the Diary Room:

'It's fascinating to see Chantelle and Preston becoming much more cunning. Chantelle is now more giggly, more dumb, more cutesy, more finger-in-the-mouth, more pulling sexy poses. Preston is very calculating. He's got sly eyes.'

I wouldn't have known where to start playing a game. I felt I just had to take each day as it came, and go along being myself. Preston and Maggot and me were talking about it, and Preston said that because we three were the youngest, the others thought we were easy pickings, and they were playing a game to get us out. But none of the three of us played a game, not at all.

But although Pete said things like this, he was still capable of being very nice. The next day, my foundation had almost completely run out. I'd been squeezing the tube extra hard for a couple of days to get the last of it, but finally there was hardly any left. Although I'd packed enough clothes for the full three weeks, I'd made a serious miscalculation with my make-up, mainly because I didn't actually expect to be there for the full run.

Pete went into the Diary Room and asked Big Brother to let me have some. How nice is that? He didn't tell me at the time, but I now know he said:

'Chantelle can't sleep. She's running out of foundation, and she's really twitchy, traumatised.'

Pete probably understood how terrible it feels to have no make-up. Anyway, in the meantime I borrowed some from Traci, but Maggot and Preston both laughed at me. They said I looked orange, like the TV presenter David Dickinson.

When we got the nomination results, and I realised I might be going home in two days' time, I said that my foundation problem wasn't so bad after all. I wasn't upset about being nominated. Like I have said a few times, I felt privileged to have lasted as long as I had, and all I could think about was that there would be a big party when I got out, and I'd see Mum and everyone else again. I could never understand why people like Traci got into such a state about being up for eviction. Of course I wanted to stay, but if my time was up, it was up. I had no idea what the public thought about me because I'd never been up for the eviction vote before. I genuinely wouldn't have minded going: I felt so grateful for having been there at all so close to the end of the show.

Pete and George had now formed a tight little partnership, and they were both vicious towards Preston and me – and the events of the day would make it all a lot worse. We were in for the Night of the Big Rows, Mark Two.

Pete said to George: 'Those two think they've got it sussed. There is nothing more annoying than a child that thinks it's got everything worked out. They're kids. I think they're too young for their age. If I was left behind in this house with children, I would combust. I'd have to take sleeping pills to get through.'

George said in the Diary Room: 'It would be a travesty if Dennis goes out. Chantelle is getting to the stage where she has gone as far as she can. She's had a terrific run. Whenever she goes out she will go to a new position in life. You will infer from that that she's the one I want to go.'

Dennis, of course, was one of his new allies, so he didn't want him to leave.

We'd all noticed a big old-fashioned telephone that had arrived in the kitchen area. Preston and I were the only two nearby when the phone rang, so I picked it up. Big Brother came on the line and told me to go to the Diary Room, taking another housemate with me, so naturally I took Preston.

In the Diary Room we were told that to win the shopping money we had to run the *Big Brother* bank, with the rest of the housemates as bankers. We were given access to our private members club, which was a room the other side of the Diary Room, where there was limitless drink, cigars, chocolates and food, and a roaring fire and leather armchairs. There was just one big snag: we were not allowed to tell the others about it, or the whole task would be a failure.

We also had to invest £10,000 and try to make a profit with it. We hadn't a clue what shares to choose from the list they gave us, but we opted for Vodafone, on the basis that everyone uses phones, and GlaxoSmithKline, a drug company because, as Preston said, 'everyone gets ill'.

Each of us was given an outfit to wear: we had bowler hats, suits and rolled umbrellas. Traci made one of Preston's eyes up with false eyelashes, so he looked like the character from *Clockwork Orange*. It seemed to irritate Pete, but I think he was just irritable anyway.

They were all irritable when Big Brother revealed our secret room to them on the screen, while we were in there. They weren't told that we had to keep it secret. At the same time, they *were* told that they would be playing two banking games, one that evening and one the next day, and it was their mission to *fail* them, but we wouldn't know that.

So this meant that the house was divided into two, with me and Preston on one side and everyone else on the other, and both sides telling lies to the other in order to pass the shopping test.

That's all it was – a stupid shopping test. But the drama that was created about it, you would have thought we were playing for much higher stakes. All Preston and me wanted was to do whatever was necessary to win the shopping money. We felt a bit guilty about having access to the extra food and drink, especially towards Maggot. But we didn't overindulge in there, simply because we didn't want the others to know about it. My one regret about the whole of my time in the house is that we didn't just relax and eat and drink everything in there!

The whole evening degenerated into a great big row

about whether Preston and I were telling lies. It was so stupid, especially as they were telling lies too.

At one point I said: 'Is this conversation going to go on all night?' If one of them had said yes, I'd have told them the truth, and blown the shopping money, without a doubt.

It's hard to believe that they could be so upset about it, especially George and Pete. As far as I was concerned, we were just having a laugh, and our part of the task was to deceive them – just as theirs was to deceive us.

The first banking task was to sort out lots of loose change into bags, and I found it hard to believe how they managed to make such a mess of it, because I had no idea they were doing it on purpose.

At least Pete's bitching was funny. He said I was 'digging a hole so deep she'll be ordering chop suey in China'.

But George was thoroughly unpleasant. He said: 'If I get the chance to repay those who took my rights away yesterday, I will. Whether it is in here or outside.'

That sounded like a threat to me. I was so shocked that a serving MP should say something like that on a TV show, actually saying something that sounded so threatening and just because we were told to play on an opposing side. I still find it unbelievable. There was so much talk about me being a child, but I don't think I was the one being childish here.

Things didn't improve after a night's sleep. Here are just a few of the edited highlights of what Pete said about me and Preston:

'Preston looks like a chimp at a chimps' tea party in that suit.'

'She's a very convincing cold liar. She could steal your purse and swear she didn't.'

'She could work as a spy. Preston has sneaky eyes.'

The second banking task was to build a tower out of blocks, and they were all trying to fail, while Preston and I were trying to get it right. I remember thinking: 'How the hell can they not build with building blocks?'

But when we were told later that we had passed the shopping task (apparently our stocks and shares had made a profit of £4.50), I just laughed at the way they had been deceiving us. It didn't matter one little bit – my attitude was 'Good for you'. I said to them, 'You bankers!'

Unfortunately, that wasn't their attitude to me and Preston – well it wasn't for George, Pete and Dennis. Maggot and Michael were fine about the fact that we had tricked them – they knew it was all in the spirit of the game. Traci didn't complain, either. She just kept her head down, and I'm not criticising her for that.

But George, Pete and Dennis – they were proper angry. It just didn't seem like the behaviour of grown men.

It was the most ridiculous day of my life. They had obviously been very jealous of us having the other private room, but what were we supposed to do? I wouldn't have minded if two of them had been in there, eating and drinking. It wasn't as though we were short of food. I just can't believe they took it so seriously.

George said he hadn't heard the phone ringing – did he

think we had made it up? They had made us lie to them, because they had insisted on asking loads of questions. If we hadn't lied, they'd have been pissed off with us for failing the task. They didn't seem to be able to see that we were all on the same side.

Pete attacked Preston verbally, and when Preston replied George interrupted with:

'Pipe down, Mr Indignation. We'll see what the viewers think of your double standards, your indignation about me, and the aplomb with which you became a lying plutocrat in your gentlemen's club . . . The long and short of it is, you are a sneak . . . You are a sneak and a liar and you are exposed to the whole country as that.'

Pete and Dennis both contributed, but it was George who was in full flow.

'You flit around, promiscuously stroking everyone. Your real character was revealed on the screen.'

I think what bugged him was that he had been exposed toadying up to Rula, and he didn't like us having something over him. George likes it when he is the one who has something over others.

In the middle of all this I told Dennis he was being petty. He went ballistic, really lost it.

He said to me: 'Where I come from, you'd get your fucking face bashed in.'

Hang on a minute, Dennis. Are you really threatening to have the brains of a twenty-two-year-old girl 'bashed in' because she argues with you on a TV show? Are you overreacting, or what? I'd hate to live where you live if people get their heads bashed in for taking part in a telly show, and doing what they have been told to do.

I was cool. I simply said: 'I'd like to see you try, Dennis.'

I wasn't frightened, although looking back I can see it was a frightening situation, having this huge man standing over me. Outside, watching their different televisions, my dad and my stepdad were both going mad, wanting to jump into the set and sort Dennis out. But I always knew we were well protected in there.

Like I said earlier, I knew one day it would be my turn to have a row with Dennis, and I'm only surprised that it took until the nineteenth day in the house for it to happen. I was prepared for it, thinking to myself: 'I'm not going to let you intimidate me.'

One thing I have learned in life is you have to stand up to bullies. I could hear Mum's voice inside my head, telling me, 'Stand up for yourself.' So I did, and it worked. Dennis tried to pretend that he hadn't really threatened me, that it was only 'general speaking', whatever that means.

George was on a rowing roll. He wasn't just gunning for us that night, he seemed ready to have an argument with anyone. I think he was really worried about being up for eviction, and that had made him think about how he was being perceived in the world outside. But if he wanted to improve his standing, he went about it in a strange way. He didn't do himself any favours.

A week and a half earlier he had been saying how much he wanted Michael to win. Now he attacked him, in the most terrible way. He said awful things about Michael, calling him 'selfish' and 'self-obsessed' and saying all he cared about 'is number one, Michael Barrymore'. He very cruelly said 'if you have any brain cells left', which sounded to me like a jibe at Michael's drinking, he said Michael only did the cooking in order to be on camera, and he sneered 'poor me, poor me, pour me another drink' at Michael. He kept on repeating it.

It was way out of order, and Preston defended Michael. I was very proud of him. He stood up for the underdog, because Michael couldn't defend himself against George, who was supported by Pete and Dennis. I just told Michael not to rise to it, and he didn't. He simply told George: 'You are going to be sorry for this, sorry for the way you have spoken to the kids.'

Pete tried to make out later that 'poor me, pour me another drink' was just an expression people use. I'd never heard it before – what would you say it about, if not about someone who drinks?

If there are rows and aggro in real life, you can walk away. But in there you are trapped, and this was the horriblest night of the lot. I couldn't understand it. We were so close to the end, so the people who were unhappy should have been happier, knowing that it was nearly over and we were close to going home.

George was always a fish out of water in there. He seemed to be trying to play the *Big Brother* game as if it was life or death, or something. Since I came out, someone suggested I should stand for Parliament against him – I'd do it for the fun of beating him! But I wouldn't have a clue what to do afterwards.

Later, the house divided into two camps more than ever

'Oh My God!'

'Chantelle, you have won Celebrity Big Brother!' – I'll remember this moment for the rest of my life.

My first premiere, *Ice Age - The Meltdown*, April 2006.

At the *Superman Returns* film premiere in July 2006.

(Clockwise)
At home in Brighton, enjoying the view.

I've been caught at the fridge – again!

Posing by my lovely new car.

Preston with his beloved coffee machine!

Admiring my husband to be – July '06.

A relaxing day at home in Brighton.

At home with Preston.

Preston eating porridge!

Meeting Prince Charles at the Prince's Trust reception at Clarence House, May 2006.

Launching an anti-bullying awareness campaign outside City Hall in London, March 2006.

Me and Jade at the 'Sport Relief Mile' charity run in Brighton, July 2006.

With Preston, James (left) and Will (right) from The Ordinary Boys at a gig in Spain.

With my mum on my hen night in London.

The happiest day
of my life.

Introducing the new
Mr and Mrs Preston.

Our first dance.

before. Preston, Michael, Maggot and me were in one camp, George, Dennis, Pete and Traci were in the other.

We were given presents that night, as a reward for winning the task – the task which had caused so much mayhem. I got a pair of roller skates. I used to roller-skate when I was a child, so it was fun doing it again. I hadn't done it for years and I wouldn't normally do it outside, but in there you can do silly things.

It did lighten the mood, although I do wonder how much pleasure George got from his gift: he was given a copy of *The Communist Manifesto*. I wonder if it said anything in there about how to treat people who are younger or weaker than you?

Chapter Twelve

Will I Stay or Will I Go?

The rhythm of the house seemed to be that after a really wild day, we would have a quiet one. We stayed in our two camps, and for the first time I had a real pang about the fact that I might be evicted the next day. Not because I minded going, but because I didn't want to leave Preston. I knew he could take care of himself, but I thought that by being there I could at least support him against George and his gang.

I knew I was very attracted to him, but I never lost sight of the fact that it couldn't be more than a friendship. I was confident the friendship would continue when we left the house, but I also knew we would never again be able to spend so much time together.

I remember thinking: 'We'll never be in this situation again if I go tomorrow.'

I felt a real pang, but I always knew that it would have to come to an end soon.

Preston said to me: 'Please don't leave me. It will be rubbish without you.' He said he had realised that although we were the two youngest, and we fooled about having a good time, apart from Maggot we were 'the only grown-ups in here'.

While we were grumbling about them, they continued to have a go at us. Dennis actually said: 'That little kid, Chantelle, is very fragile.'

That was a real liberty. I'd shown him the night before that I was strong enough to take him on. There was a debating game, but it didn't bring us closer together. George took it seriously, but most of the rest of us just had a laugh.

One really strange thing happened that day. The shopping was delivered, and it was great to find that Big Brother had taken pity on me and delivered some foundation, two tubes. Just as we were opening the shopping I saw Dennis taking one of them and putting it into his pocket.

'Oi, that's mine,' I said, and he handed it over without a fuss. But it was weird. Maybe he was just trying to be horrible. He had a habit of pocketing other people's cigarettes, too.

The next day was eviction day, and I did feel excited. Whatever happened, things were going to change, and I could well be going home. I imagined Mum and Dean getting ready to come to Elstree, as I knew they'd be there just in case I came out. Dad and my friend Rachael were also there, but I didn't know that then.

George said in the morning that there might be two

evictions: we could all see that there were a lot of us, eight altogether, in the house, and it needed to be thinned out for the end, which was only fifty-two hours away (Michael worked it out).

We were distracted because we had to make a movie about the *Big Brother* house. We all had to play other housemates. I chose Dennis, as I didn't like him so I didn't mind taking the mick out of him. Maybe that's how Pete felt, too, when he chose Jodie – but he went way, way over the top. I didn't like it at all, and I know he wouldn't have done it if she had been in the house. It was out of order.

I said to Preston: 'They wouldn't have done it if she had been here.'

The fact that I was upset was clear to the others, and Pete had a real go at me behind my back.

Talking about me and Jodie he said: 'They'll go out and do topless modelling tomorrow . . . Let's face it, she can't sing, she's never made a record. What's she going to do? Topless modelling. Of course I hope she gets voted out. She's getting fried alive.'

He really got into it, and came back to it again: 'Have you noticed her striking poses? Isn't it like a topless model? Couldn't you see her in a magazine?'

The only time he said it to my face was at the end of the filming of our movie, when, as Jodie, he said to Maggot, who was playing me: 'Come on, we can do topless modelling together.'

He was taking it too far, and I didn't find it funny. To be accused of topless modelling is not an insult to me, in fact I'm proud of having done it. But his whole tone and his aggressive impersonation of Jodie was upsetting. I still couldn't understand why they took it all so seriously.

Preston agreed. He said: 'Pete went right over the lines of decency and taste. It was incredibly funny to watch, but painful.'

I couldn't even see it as funny. I forgave Pete a great deal in that house, because he made me laugh. But this was all too over the top. I didn't say anything, but you could see from my face that I felt hurt and shocked. I thought he could never upset me, but when I saw on the video what he said to Dennis later that day, I was a bit shocked.

'She's quite a tough girl. There's a look that comes into her eyes, isn't there? I knew she was too cute when she first came in. There's no way she could get across the road if she was like that. If I was Preston's girlfriend I'd be right at the end of that catwalk saying, "Hi, Blondie, first let me help you remove those hair extensions." Then I'd be out there waiting for him. And I certainly wouldn't want him taking phone calls from her. I'd bust his mobile right through his skull. Not because you can keep someone, but just for your own amusement and revenge.'

I don't think he meant it. I think the situation of being in that house made him say things like that. Perhaps he was jealous because at least I could do topless modelling!

In the Diary Room, Michael said some really sweet things about me. He was talking about those who were up for eviction that night, and he said he thought George had overreacted to being nominated, and his attitude was 'I feel like crap and I'm going to make you feel like crap'.

He then said: 'Chantelle has the perfect attitude to

eviction. Whether it is naivety – it's all new to her – I hope she keeps her naivety. It think it's a good quality and she should keep it. She's really, really excited.'

When Big Brother asked him if he had learned anything from my behaviour he said: 'Absolutely. She's reminded me to keep things simple and to appreciate every minute we have in this business we call show.'

He was right, I was very excited about the eviction. I changed into my eviction outfit, the champagne-coloured dress that was the same as the black one I wore on the way in, but I put my black dressing gown over it. I was completely ready to go, but I wanted to save the impact of my dress for when my name was called and I did leave.

It's strange being up for nomination at a normal eviction – you don't know whether you are going or not. On the final night, at least you know you will be leaving even if you don't know in what order, so you can prepare for something definite.

When Davina's voice came into the house, I could hardly contain my excitement.

'The next person to leave the *Celebrity Big Brother* house is . . . George.'

I was overwhelmed, because I'd been sure it would be me. You always imagine you are the one who will go – it's safer that way, so that you aren't disappointed when it happens. It's just a coping mechanism. I had no idea what the public thought about me, and because George was a famous politician, and Dennis was world-famous, I thought I was the likeliest choice to go. Also, I'd been thinking about Mum and the rest of the family being out there waiting for me, and I was quite excited about seeing them. But when it wasn't me, I knew they would be as glad as I was that I was staying in.

I was relieved to see the back of George, the troublemaker-in-chief. In his interview with Davina he said the house was 'boring and turgid' – I think he just said that to make himself sound superior. He also said I was 'as sharp as a tack'. That was a turnabout! I think he'd realised I wasn't the stupid uneducated girl he had patronised for all that time in there. George was horrible to me and tried to shout me down when I confronted him. And I wasn't the only one he treated like this. The party he represents is the Respect Party, but like I said in the house, where he's concerned, it should have the three letters D I S in front of the name.

I still had a feeling that something else would happen. Although we all knew there was a chance of another eviction, Dennis said when George went: 'I'm going to be here to the end.' I wasn't so confident, and I reapplied my lip gloss just in case.

Then we heard Davina's voice again, and this time Dennis went.

I felt very happy – now the two I most disliked had gone. I knew Mum would be so proud of me, and she wouldn't have minded a wasted journey to Elstree. It felt weird that she was just outside, so close, but that didn't upset me because I knew I would see her in two days' time, whatever happened.

When he was talking to Davina, Dennis said Preston and me didn't do anything around the house. That was great, coming from him. Dennis was the rudest, most arrogant man I have ever met in my entire life. I never really chatted to him the whole time we were there: maybe he felt it was an insult that a non-celebrity was in there.

Michael gave me a huge hug when Dennis walked out, and so did Maggot and Preston. We were all shell-shocked, and there was still a worry about what was going to happen. There were six of us left – Big Brother had never had such a large number for a final night.

I was gobsmacked to have won against George and Dennis.

Preston said: 'It's so obvious, you're lovely.'

Maggot said it was because I didn't shout at people and nick their fags, and Michael and Preston agreed that the public had seen the way they bullied us. I didn't care what the reason was: I was there to the end.

We had a premiere party for the movie, and some lovely evening dresses came in for me and Traci to choose from. Mine was beautiful, in cerise pink – I wish I could have kept it. Surprisingly, Pete chose a suit, not a dress.

I was in the bedroom taking off my eviction outfit when I had a conversation with Pete, which I thought was nice, but which I now can see was two-faced. He joked that I'd stayed in because I was a 'slapper' and he said when I left 'people will be chucking new clothes at you. I hate to be a smart-arse, but I could have told you when your name came up, "She ain't going anywhere." '

We all drank too much at the party, which made a lovely end to the evening. Traci, Preston and me went into the Diary Room together and had a drunken conversation with

Big Brother, who asked us how we felt about the evictions. I said I was very happy, and Preston said he was, too. Traci said she was 'discombobulated', but added she was happy, too. I think she had been thrown by Dennis going, as they spent a lot of time together.

But she was very sweet about me and Preston. She said it seemed 'like you have lived this happiness before. Last night I said to Maggot that you two seem so happy and adorable together, and it doesn't seem like a new thing. It's like you have been doing it for a while, before you got into the *Big Brother* house. I feel you ought to get together and be married with a ring, I hope I'm there. If this is a new relationship – WOW!'

We both tried to take the heat out of it.

'It's just that we get on with each other.' Preston said.

'We trust each other,' I added.

We were all a bit the worse for drink, and it ended with me and Traci both kissing Preston who said: 'I feel like I'm going to explode.'

Now that I knew I was staying to the end, I put all thoughts of the outside world out of my mind. I was just glad to still be there, to still be with Preston. I knew by this time that I really fancied him, and deep down I hoped he felt the same way. But I also knew that we were on camera all the time, and that he had a girlfriend. So nothing could possibly happen between us, and when we left the house he would go back to his relationship. I couldn't allow myself to think about there being anything serious between us, I had to keep it as light as possible, even deep inside myself. I never dwelt on what it would be like outside, when I couldn't be with him all the time.

We spent two more days in the house, and it was a very happy time. I was so determined to enjoy every moment. Everyone who was there knew they had made it; everyone was, in that sense, a winner. And we all knew we were soon going to see our friends and families, so there was that to look forward to.

We were willing the time to pass, and we sat around for hours just talking. It was great that all the rows were over, and nobody was having a go at anybody else. Even Pete seemed more relaxed, without George and Dennis winding him up.

On the final day Big Brother treated us to a huge hamper full of pampering products: lovely shower gels, creams, shampoos, etc. There was loads of food, plenty of coffee for those who missed it badly whenever we ran out, lots of cigarettes for the smokers. Nobody had anything to whinge about.

I can remember looking at the clock on the cooker and thinking: 'Come on, come on.' I just wanted to get on with it.

We all had to go into the Diary Room for one last time. I said I thought Preston would win.

'He's a really nice, genuine person. I think there's probably a lot of girls out there who have fallen in love with him and he'll break a lot of hearts when he turns round and tells them he's got a girlfriend. To genuinely be a nice person is a nice thing, so I think he will win.'

I meant everything I said – I did think he was a really nice person. Looking back at the videotapes of the show, I think everyone watching must have realised how nice he was. Of course, I was one of the girls who had fallen in love with him, and I just felt lucky to have been able to get to know him in person, rather than just on the television screen. More than anything else I wanted him to at least be my friend when we left.

Maggot told Big Brother he wanted to win. He was very honest about it: he wanted to make some money, and get his band back into the headlines. Michael chose Maggot to win. He said he hadn't had any expectations about *Big Brother*, but that he had really enjoyed it.

Pete said he would like to see Michael win, because he felt Michael needed to feel 'mass adulation and love'.

About me he said: 'Chantelle would like to win it, and I don't think that's a bad character reference. I think she's a cold-eyed shark and she wants pop stardom now.'

Really, Pete, you were reading far too much into everything! I never wanted a pop career, whatever the press outside were suggesting. And as for being a 'cold-eyed shark', I'm a bit shocked that he could still be so vicious towards me.

Preston said he would like to win, having got this far.

'It's never been a competition, it's never been about that, but if someone says you can win it or not win it, I'd rather win it.

'At the same time, I really want Chantelle to win it. In fact, I'd rather Chantelle win it, because she wasn't a celebrity when she came in.'

Traci gave a funny little speech, like a beauty queen saying what her own attributes are. I suppose it's quite American, but we wouldn't do that sort of thing and I found it a bit embarrassing when I watched the video.

She said: 'I'm a great person. I do listen, I do care, I've done my share of the housework and I do care about people's hearts and feelings. I'm fun to be around, exciting, a good family member, someone who makes you smile.'

It was such hot air. It was different for me from the others, because they were in there to win and I was there just to be on *Big Brother*. If it had been a normal *Big Brother*, probably I'd have been wanting to win. But I felt I shouldn't have been there, and so I had achieved everything I wanted, anyway.

So when Davina started announcing who was going, every time we heard her voice I was ready to get up and go. The first one out was Traci, so her little electioneering speech hadn't done any good. Although she was there to the final day, I never got to know Traci. I don't think she knows herself. It may be that whole LA thing, where all they care about is their hair, the shape of their nose and their tans, and perhaps that means there isn't time left to worry about anything else. Or maybe she was just very guarded. In all that time, she never let anyone into her life, and I can't tell you what sort of person she is.

The evictions came thick and fast, and we hardly had time to recover from one before the next one was announced. Second to go that night was Pete, and then after him, Preston. This really shocked me: I was so sure he would go the distance. I felt I was going to burst into tears when he left, but I was also so glad it happened on the day that I was leaving: I would have been devastated if he had left earlier in the show. As he left we hugged, but there was no time to say anything. It was literally a few seconds from the announcement to him being out, and at that stage all everyone thinks about is what is waiting for them outside. We knew we would see each other soon.

After he left I went into the toilet. I didn't really need to go, I just wanted to sort myself out in my head. While I was thinking it all through, Preston was being interviewed by Davina. His girlfriend was there, in the crowd, but he still said nice things about me.

'She's gorgeous, she's a little angel. We're just mates, really good mates. I'm flirty anyway, and I started flirting with someone and didn't realise I was going to be really good mates with them, so it sort of crossed over. There's nothing between me and Chantelle but a loving friendship.'

Then Davina asked him: 'If you were single, would you?'

He replied: 'No comment.'

He also said that he had learned a lot about trust in the house, having started off trusting everyone. But he said he'd rather be disappointed than never trust anyone.

Davina then announced the fourth person to leave that night: Maggot. It was not very fair for him, because after his name was announced he was told he had to stay with me and Michael for half an hour, during the break between the two live programmes. I'd have hated that, I'd have wanted to get on with it.

I can't remember that any of us talked much. Michael pointed out that it was going to be me and him at the end, and we had been the first two in at the beginning. I hadn't thought of that until he said it. We weren't allowed out of the seating area, so we couldn't pop into the kitchen to make a cup of tea – not that I would have wanted one. We had water, but I stopped drinking anything about three hours before the programme started because I didn't want to be uncomfortable, wanting to go to the loo during my eviction.

Michael and I held hands really tight when Davina's voice came on again, and looked at each other.

'The winner of *Celebrity Big Brother 2006* is . . .'

Davina held the pause so long Michael asked me if I was OK, and I just managed to nod.

'. . . CHANTELLE!!!'

I was so shocked, flabbergasted. I'd felt sure Michael would get it.

'Oh my God!' I said. 'Are you sure?'

Michael hugged me and again asked me if I was OK. I clung to him for a moment, and then Davina's voice told me to stay in the house, and him to leave.

I didn't know what to do. I was on my own for about ten minutes, I suppose, while Michael went out, to huge cheers from everyone, and did his interview with Davina. I learned afterwards that Preston was the first housemate to leave to universal cheers – everyone else had faced a mixture of cheers and boos. From Preston onwards, it was cheering all the way.

While Michael was telling Davina that I was 'an absolute example of what a celebrity is meant to be – cool and laid-back', I was feeling anything but cool and laid-back. I was in complete shock, wandering around the house. Apparently I said 'Oh my God' more than forty times, and I fiddled with my hair the whole time. I couldn't wait to see Mum and everyone, and I tried to imagine how they were feeling.

I was desperate for someone to talk to: it felt so lonely in there, in that house which had been so crowded and busy for three weeks. I think Big Brother sensed how I was feeling because the voice came in and said: 'Congratulations, Chantelle.'

I said: 'Thank you,' but BB didn't say anything else and I didn't really feel any calmer. Apparently 56.4% of the final vote had been for me, which I still find astonishing.

At last, the voice of Big Brother came on again:

'Chantelle, you have won *Celebrity Big Brother*, please leave the *Big Brother* house.'

I had to walk through the house, and all I could think about was my family out there, and that I would see them very soon. But when the door opened, it was impossible to see anything: I was blinded by the lights, and over-whelmed by the deafening roar. The fireworks were the most spectacular I have ever seen, there were cameras flashing, people screaming. It seemed completely unreal.

After Davina took me to pose in front of the cameras, I spotted Mum and the rest of them – Dean, Dad and Rachael

– in the crowd. It was so good. I couldn't talk to them or touch them, but I screamed 'I love you' and they yelled it back.

I really didn't feel cold, but everyone else was wearing heavy jackets and fur coats. I told Davina that all I could feel was excitement and happiness. When Davina asked me how I felt I said: 'Words can't say. I can't believe it's real. Is this another task or something?'

Even then, at this wonderful stage, there was something in the back of my head saying that it must be a trick, because things like this don't happen to promotions girls from Essex with 8p in the bank.

Davina showed me a load of front pages from newspapers, with my picture all over them. It was so weird. I knew the press always made a big splash about *Big Brother*, but I didn't expect half as much fuss as that.

Then she said: 'Let's talk about Preston. You keep saying you don't fancy him.'

I said: 'No, I don't.' He has teased me about this since, but at the time I was still not admitting even to myself that there was something serious between us. Of course I fancied him, but I would much rather have lied than say something that might have caused problems between him and his girlfriend.

'I will tell you the God's honest truth. I knew I liked Preston a little bit more, but it wasn't until the Saturday afternoon that I realised it was because I trusted him, and to be able to trust someone in there is a really, really big thing. I just trust him and genuinely like him.'

I told her I hoped to keep in touch with everyone

because 'what went on inside the house stays in the house. If it had been real life, things wouldn't have happened and we wouldn't have found out how people really are . . .'

Davina said that if we all knew what our best friends say behind our backs we wouldn't have any best friends. But, actually, the people I was friends with in there, like Preston and Maggot, never said anything bad behind my back, and with Michael it was only a silly couple of days when Jodie upset him. Having watched the videos, I have been shocked by some of the things people said, but my faith in my judgement remains the same. The people I instinctively liked turned out to be true friends.

It was when Davina asked me what I was going to do next that I turned to Mum, who yelled: 'LIVE THE DREAM.'

That was exactly what I intended to do, but when Davina said they would be giving me £25,000 in prize money, I really felt I was in a dream.

'Are you sure?' I said again. I hadn't thought about money at all and I would cheerfully have done it for nothing.

Davina said: 'You are living the dream. You went in as a non-celebrity and you have come out as a celebrity with £25,000. Chantelle, all I can say, from the heart, from me, please, please don't change.'

I said: 'Never will. I don't know how to change.'

Davina finished the show with the words: 'You are lovely, and that's why you are sitting here. You've been an incredible celebrity housemate.'

And then she took me down the catwalk to see the

vous: I was far too excited for nerves. The press were fine: they seemed most interested in whether I would form a band called Kandy Floss and release 'I Want It Right Now'. I never had any plans to do that – as you know, I can't sing a note, and I'd only have done it if it was for charity.

After meeting the press I had to do a quick interview for *Big Brother's Big Mouth*. I have no idea what questions I was asked, it's all a complete blur. So is the after-show party, although I do remember meeting up with all the production team, who hugged and kissed me. I didn't drink much: I was perfectly high and excited enough without the help of alcohol! I know Preston was there, because I caught a glimpse of him, but I didn't speak to any of the other housemates. I guess they were there, but I didn't see them.

Then we all climbed into cars to be whisked away. Dad and Rachael were taken back to Wickford, but Mum, Dean and I went to a fabulous hotel not too far away from Elstree. It was so good to see them. We stayed up till 5 a.m. I wasn't a bit tired, and I just wanted to talk and talk to them. We went over everything: I told them about life in the house and they told me what had been happening outside. It suddenly hit me that I was hungry – I hadn't felt like eating earlier in the day. The only vegetarian food I could get at that time of night was a tomato sandwich.

I only had about two hours' sleep, because I had a very busy day ahead. Our hotel rooms were arranged along a veranda, and as I walked to Mum and Dean's room the next morning I saw all the newspapers left outside guests' rooms, and my face was on all the front pages, even the posh ones like *The Times* and the *Telegraph*. The best headline was in the Sun: 'NOBODY WINS BIG BRUV.'

The nicest – and weirdest – thing that happened that morning was when I woke up. I switched on the TV in my hotel bedroom, and there on the screen was Preston, singing his hit 'Boys Will be Boys'. I'd woken up every morning for over three weeks seeing him, so it felt kinda normal to see him again, but weird not being able to look across the room and see him lying in his bed. It was the first time I properly heard him sing: he'd sung the same song in the house, but I was so worried about my own performance on that occasion that I didn't properly appreciate any of the others. The next day I asked Mum to get me his CD when she went shopping. It was really nice hearing his voice – I love his music.

When Pete asked me in the house what I intended doing afterwards, I genuinely thought that after a bit of fuss in the newspapers, I'd be looking for work again. But winning made a huge difference, and I was (I was told) in great demand for interviews and photo sessions. The first thing I had to do was fix myself up with an agent to handle all the uproar. Endemol, the TV company, had arranged a series of meetings for me with different agencies that morning, and I was very happy with the first one I met. John Noel is Davina's agent, and he also looks after Jade Goody and lots of the people who have been in *Big Brother*. I felt comfortable with him, and I was introduced to Sally Andrews, who takes care of my TV work, and Katherine Lister who takes care of all my press interviews and photoshoots. They have both become good friends.

I did have a letter from one of the modelling agencies

whose books I was on before I went into the house. They set out what they could do for me. I had a laugh – they hadn't done anything for me before, now they wanted part of my success. I hadn't heard from them for ages, but now they thought I could make some money for them they were in touch. I ignored the letter.

It was a mad day. There were paparazzi photographers waiting for us when we finished the meeting, and they tailed us to the house in Islington where I did my first official photoshoot as the *Celebrity Big Brother* winner. It was for *OK!* magazine and the Express group of newspapers. I couldn't believe it: I was going to be on the front of *OK!*, the magazine full of glamorous people I had always envied. It all felt completely unreal.

Despite being very tired, I loved the photo session, which went on until late at night. I'd never done anything like it in my modelling career, and I really enjoyed it. I had to do separate interviews, for the magazine, the *Daily Star* and the *Daily Star Sunday*. Mum and Dean were with me, and they were exhausted, too. At one point we didn't know where Dean was, then we found him asleep in one of the bedrooms. We left him until it was time to go home, at about 1 a.m. I was running on adrenalin – I could have kept going. When the photographer took the last shot I was like: 'Is that it?'

It was only when the shoot was over, going home in the car, that I suddenly felt deflated and started to miss Preston, who had been my constant companion for three weeks. I burst into tears and Mum put her arms around me.

'I just miss him,' was all I could say between sobs.

'I know you do,' was all she could say.

I'd been with him every day, and now he was gone. But at least I knew I would see him the next day at the studios for the reunion on *Big Brother's Little Brother*.

I fell asleep as soon as I got into my own, familiar pink bedroom in Wickford. I was so tired I didn't have time to think about the whole amazing day. When I woke the next morning I was in my own surroundings, and for a split second I forgot everything that had happened, as if my life was just the same as it always had been. Then I realised, and the happiness flooded over me again.

It was another early start, for *Big Brother's Little Brother*, with Dermot O'Leary. He lived up to my expectations – he was really lovely. The other housemates were all there, and I managed to chat briefly to Preston. Seeing him there took my breath away, and I think I realised then just how much in love with him I was. We were all saying how crazy it was, and how big the programme had been. I didn't have time for a personal chat with any of them, even Preston.

As soon as the driver dropped me back at home, I went to bed again. I was so, so tired. There were stacks of cards and flowers – Mum was running out of vases to put them in. I was particularly pleased with a lovely bouquet from my friends Emma and Louise. There were free gifts of make-up and beauty products. And Mum had a two-foot-high pile of newspaper cuttings for me, which I haven't read to this day. She's put them all in boxes and stored them away: for when I have time to look at them.

The doorbell never stopped ringing, with friends

popping round and reporters and photographers camped outside. Mum and Dean did a great job of keeping them at bay. They didn't mind the intrusion: I think they secretly loved it. Gregg told me that he was really proud of me, which was great.

One of the weirdest things I did in the first couple of days was to put my bank card in a hole in the wall bank machine. I just asked for a statement. The piece of paper popped out and it read: £25,000.8. I just looked at it in disbelief. It felt as though the only bit that was really mine was the 8p. It was completely amazing. I was so grateful. I've never had that sort of money.

I desperately needed to go to the hairdresser's: it was top of my list of things to be done when I came out of the house. But there was no time. Monday was the day of the wrap party. There's a tradition in television and filming that when the show is over there is a party to celebrate: 'It's a wrap', the words used when the last shot has been filmed.

I also had to appear on Graham Norton's show, *The Bigger Picture*. So Mum and I got up early and made a quick dash to the Lakeside shopping centre, where I found a nice dress. Dean came with us: he described himself as our minder. There weren't too many people about, but a few came up and asked me to sign my autograph or have my picture taken. Nowadays, with everyone having a camera on their mobile phones, they'd rather take a picture than get a signature. Being asked was the funniest thing. As we walked along I'd hear people whispering, 'It's Chantelle – it is, it really is!' It was mental, knowing that everyone knew who I was.

Mum and Dean both took some time off work to be with me in those early, mad, days. Mum became a bit of a celebrity herself, with people asking to take her picture. One person even took a picture of 'Chantelle's mum's car'. When she was doing normal things, like going to the supermarket, she'd hear people whispering behind her: 'That's Chantelle's mum.' Mum loved it. She was just so happy that I'd got everything I wanted.

Dad used to hear people in the back of his cab talking about me. Sometimes he'd tell them I was his daughter, sometimes he just listened. He says he never heard anyone say anything bad about me. He was bursting with pride. He says he always knew I was a star, but now everybody else could see it, too!

The dress I bought was very me – lots of bright colours. It was made by Guess, and it was a brown background with the word Guess in pink, green and yellow all over it. It had a halter-neck and it came to below the knee.

The other guests on Graham Norton's programme were Carol Thatcher, Ben Fogle and Ruby Wax. Carol Thatcher was really lovely, and chatted to me in the dressing room. Ben Fogle seemed nice, although I didn't get chance to talk to him. But Ruby Wax seemed very hostile. She kept on about 'fifteen minutes of fame' and she said 'We'll see how long!' as a reference to my career. I thought: 'At least let me have my moment, for God's sake. Don't try to turn the light out the minute it has been switched on.'

Graham Norton himself was lovely and made me feel very comfortable. With him, what you see is what you get: he's exactly the same on or off camera. As for me, I didn't feel a bit nervous being in a TV studio for the first time properly. I felt I'd come home, it was everything I expected it to be. I was happy to find I could do it and wanted to do it.

As soon as I left the studio, the driver whisked me away to the wrap party. There were loads of photographers: as I walked into the club, near Piccadilly Circus, it was like a sea of white light all around me, with so many flashes going off I was blinded. I was one of the first arrivals: there were no other housemates, and Mum and Dean and Rachael hadn't arrived. The production people all chatted to me, then Maggot arrived, and Rula. I was really pleased to see them, but before long the place was packed and it was so noisy it was difficult to chat to anyone. All the housemates except Jodie and George were there. Jodie and I still haven't had time to meet up since being in the house, because we've both been so busy.

I didn't have much to drink (which was funny, because the press all had pictures of me coming out of the party looking tired, and they wrote stories about me suggesting I'd had too much to drink; I hadn't, but I was *really*, *really* tired). I kept thinking: I want to remember these days for ever, I don't want anything to cloud my memory.

Preston came with his manager and we were able to have a very brief chat. I was so pleased to see him. But everyone wanted to talk to the housemates, and it was so noisy, which meant there was no chance for a one to one chat. We didn't exchange numbers, and afterwards I felt gutted, because I thought I would never see him again. I didn't think about being his girlfriend, because I had no right to think like that. But I knew that I really, really missed him and I felt empty inside. One night when I was looking through a magazine in bed I saw his picture, and I kissed him goodnight – I've only recently confessed to him that I did that.

It was hard, because Preston was the one person everyone wanted to ask me about. It was the question on every interviewer's lips, and out of respect for him I couldn't tell anyone that I found him really attractive.

I remember going to bed after the wrap party and there was a great big bit of me that was so happy, but there was another bit that was very unhappy. I knew there was something missing, something important.

The next official function I did was very weird: I presented an award at the Channel 4 Political Awards. Me, who had only ever met one politician, and that was George Galloway! I had to hand over the award for the rising star, which went to a Conservative MP, Michael Gove. Jamie Oliver won the Most Inspiring Political Figure Award, although he was not there in person to collect it, and appeared by video link. The comedian Arabella Weir was on my table. My agent Sally came with me, thank goodness, because I didn't know anybody.

I left as early as possible, as I had to be up at five the next morning to be interviewed on *GMTV*. I ended up blurting out the winner of the political award, which was supposed to be a secret because the programme recorded the night before hadn't been aired yet. I don't think it mattered – it would be a different audience. Again, I felt completely at home in the studio – I didn't want to leave! Mum and Sally came with me, and as we were walking along the corridor afterwards we came face to face with the actor Martin Kemp. He said: 'Hi, all right?' I couldn't believe he knew who I was. All I could say was, 'Oh my God, it's you!' Not exactly cool, was I? But he said: 'Well done. Congratulations. You did really well.'

It happened all the time in those early days: I just couldn't take in that half the country knew me and knew my name, and it was particularly surreal when they were famous themselves.

After *GMTV* I had to be photographed for a promotion for the Euromillions lottery rollover. We had paparazzi following our car again, and I had to lie down in the back because I was still under contract to *OK!* magazine. I remember one of the paps on a motorbike caught up with our car at traffic lights and drew up alongside. He peered in and I sat up – if I was going to have a snatch picture taken, I wasn't going to be lying down!

Life was so hectic and chaotic that I was living on sandwiches or not eating at all. But at least I now had a couple of days off. By this time, someone had given us each other's numbers, and Preston and I had started talking by phone and texting each other, which felt good: I hated not being in touch with him. They were just friendly, jokey texts, keeping up with what was happening to each other. But when he rang me to tell me he had proposed to his girlfriend, Camille, I felt as though I had been hit by a bus, or beaten up. But I knew I had no right to have feelings for him, other than as a friend so I simply said how pleased I was for him. Mum knew how I felt, and my friend Rachael suspected – I think everyone suspected. But I couldn't own up to it. I had to be pleased for Preston, because all I wanted was the best for him. Secretly, I cried at night.

I wanted him in my life, and if the only way to have him was as a friend, that would have to do. But I would not have kept in touch with him if Camille had not said it was OK for him to talk to me. I was always worried about phoning him, but he assured me it was all right.

For me, it was the first time in my life that I had ever been properly in love. I loved every bit of him. I'd never felt anything like it before. One thing about living together in the *Big Brother* house, you really get to know each other inside out. I knew I would never, ever, in a million years, meet anyone that good. He could make me laugh, but he was also caring and – well, just perfect. I haven't got words to say it. The feelings are deeper than anything I dreamed could be possible.

It was a difficult time, because the newspapers were full of his engagement. I congratulated him, and tried to sound as though I was pleased. In one way I was: I love him enough to just want him to be happy. But gradually over the next few days we both admitted in our phone calls that we were really missing each other. We both said it was only the friendship we missed – we didn't express our true feelings, and I didn't influence his decision to end his engagement, it was between them. I always behaved with respect towards his relationship.

But the engagement only lasted for five days, much to the delight of the newspapers, who made a massive deal about it. I felt very sorry for them both, especially his girl-friend. I never, ever wanted her to get hurt. But you cannot escape falling in love, it is something that happens without you choosing it.

We never confessed our feelings for each other until he was single. He rang me and told me he had broken it off before it appeared in the papers. He wanted to warn me, because he knew the press would go mad and that I might have to deal with them too. Inside I was jumping for joy, but I hated that someone else was sad. I hated it. I felt so bad. I've been in that position and it's horrible. I never meant to cause any hurt, and I'm really sorry if I did.

At the same time this was a wonderful conversation for me because this was when our friendly, flirty chats started to become something else. We finally dared to admit that we were desperate to see each other.

While this turmoil was going on, I still had to smile and be my usual, giggly self for the television cameras. Endemol decided to make a series of programmes about my life after *Big Brother*. Guess what they called it? *Living the Dream*. So while everything in my personal life was all over the place, I had a camera crew going everywhere with me.

They joined me the day after Preston's engagement was announced. I'd had a couple of days off, but I found it impossible to rest. With all the excitement I was getting up early in the morning. The postman was still delivering loads of cards and letters, the florist's van was always in our road bringing more flowers, and there were all my friends to catch up with. I rang Nan and Grandad, but I didn't even have time to go and see them. There were endless phone calls, some of them a bit peculiar. I had to change my number, because lots of people had it from before the house and some of the calls I received weren't very nice.

There were always photographers outside the house, sometimes five or six of them. Mum wasn't bothered about them being there: she used to feel sorry for them and take them mugs of tea. Mum and I tried to go shopping at Bluewater, and there were so many people calling out 'Chantelle'. Lots of little girls came up to have pictures taken with me, which I found really nice. Not too long ago, I was one of those girls. I ended up just buying a T-shirt and a belt.

It was good to be so busy: it would have been much harder coping with my feelings about Preston if I had had time to dwell on it.

The camera crew flew with me to Dublin where I appeared on *The Brendan Courtney Show*. Brendan is a big name in Ireland and his chat show is very popular. He's a great guy – we've kept in touch. I used all my trademark phrases on his show: 'lovin' it', 'how nice is that', 'mental, innit'. They're not things I say deliberately – I've always said them, I don't notice them. It was my first time in Ireland, but I didn't have time to see anything apart from the hotel and the TV studio, which was a shame.

It was a gorgeous, luxurious hotel. I've become used to fantastic hotels in the last few months. I'd never been in anything like them before. I remember lying back on a huge bed and thinking: 'I had nothing, and now I've got everything.' I think I will always stay grounded, I'll never be silly with my money, because I can remember what it was like to have none.

The girls who worked on *Living the Dream* have become really good friends. It was easier to talk to them about what was happening because they were going through it all with me. It's much harder to talk to someone who doesn't know what it's like. Also, it was hard in these mad days at the beginning to keep up with my old friends, although I managed to call and text them, and they all understood.

The girls from the production company were living the dream with me. It became one of our jokes:

'Stop trying to get in on my dream!' I'd say.

On the day Preston split up with his girlfriend I was shooting some scenes in the street for *The Friday Night Project*, Channel 4's programme that was being presented that week by Jamie Oliver. I went to Romford and had to run up and down the street pretending that I mistook members of the public for celebrities. It was a real laugh, and I enjoyed doing it. I love the whole presenting thing. Everyone was so nice, and, as usual, I had endless photographs taken with my arms round complete strangers. Being so busy was good for me, but at every spare moment I'd be thinking about Preston, wondering where he was and what he was doing, and going over in my head everything we'd said the moment we had both confessed to missing each other and wanting to meet up.

Later in the day I was filming the trails (the short bits promoting the programme) for *Living the Dream*. For the shoot they'd hired an amazing flat where everything was white and minimal. The bath was see-through. It was very modern and trendy, and I liked it – but I couldn't have lived there. We were all frightened to touch anything in case we marked it.

The following day I had another *OK!* magazine shoot and interview booked in, and I was desperate to get my hair done for it. So that evening the car took me straight to the salon in Southend, where Warren opened up specially for me. He was so pleased to see me – my extensions had put his salon on the map. But he had a real go at me for constantly fiddling with them. He said he watched me in the *Big Brother* house and he was shouting at me on the screen: 'Leave your extensions alone, Chantelle!' He has always told me that my hair is too blonde, but I didn't want to change it then – though I did go for real hair extensions instead of the acrylic ones, for a softer look.

It was 4 a.m. before I got home, which meant another night with only a couple of hours' sleep. Then it was off to London for another hectic day. The photoshoot was funny, because *OK!* had brought in some lookalikes, so they took a picture of me having tea with the Queen, Prince William, and Posh and Becks. How cool is that?

I really enjoy fashion shoots. I love trying on the clothes and the shoes, and having my make-up and hair done for me. It took all day, and in the evening I had to film *The Friday Night Project*. I met Jamie Oliver, the comedian Alan Carr and Tara Palmer-Tomkinson. It was all good silly fun, and I had a quick chat with Tara in the dressing room. The rest of them were going out for an Indian afterwards, but I was so tired I just went home.

Preston and I were talking on the phone and texting each other, and we did finally admit that we had feelings for each other. It was a very tender, romantic time, but we were also both very busy and we still hadn't seen each other. Whenever my phone beeped with a text I was so excited, hoping that it would be Preston.

The next day I did my first paid work as a TV presenter, when I filmed the links for E4 Music, which was a compilation of some of my best tracks for a girls' night out. The producer had selected the music, but it was all great, the kind of thing I like, girlie dance music, and I well enjoyed doing it, although for the first time I felt butterflies in my tummy.

They told me I was a natural – I remember saying, 'I'm not a natural blonde, but I really hope I'm a natural TV presenter.'

As well as the E4 camera crew, I had the *Living the Dream* crew with me, too, so it was all a bit mental.

Straight away afterwards I went for a media training session with Matthew Wright, the broadcaster and journalist. It was arranged by my agent, to give me a few tips on how to handle questions I didn't want to answer. Matthew taught me how not to dry up with embarrassment, and how to turn the question round on the interviewer. It came in handy the very next day!

It was after that I went to meet Preston at his brother Alex's house in London. It was a big moment, the first time I had seen him since the wrap party, and since all the drama with his engagement. I was very excited and very nervous. I'd gone straight from work, so I hadn't had time to worry about what I was wearing. When he opened the door he was so cute, even more than I remembered. All my nerves disappeared straight away: it felt so natural being with him. We'd spoken on the phone about being together, and we decided that night that we were completely right for each other. The first proper kiss was unbelievable. I could have cried with happiness, and I wanted it to go on for ever. That night we said the words 'I love you' for the first time, and agreed that we wanted to be together properly. But we decided we wouldn't let anyone know we were together just yet.

I can't explain how lovely it was to be with him. Anyone who has been completely and totally in love will know what I'm talking about. We just couldn't get enough of each other: we knew we had to be together. He made me feel like an eleven-year-old kid, I was so giggly around him. I felt so happy, completely. Everything was right: I'd won *Celebrity Big Brother*, my life was a round of photoshoots and trying on lovely clothes, I was earning more money than I had dreamed of. And I had Preston. How good is that?

Chapter Fourteen

True Happiness

Matthew Wright's tips saved me the next morning, when I was on Vernon Kay's Radio 1 show. He asked me if I'd slept with Preston. A day earlier and I could honestly have answered no but now . . . Anyway, it was certainly a question I wanted to avoid.

So I did what Matthew said, and I turned it round on the interviewer.

'Have you?' I asked, then collapsed in giggles as I realised I had just asked Vernon Kay if he had slept with Preston. It may have all sounded very silly, but it got me off the hook, and I didn't have to answer the question.

While I was at Radio 1 I bumped into Brian Dowling, the winner of *Big Brother 2*. He was really friendly, funny and bubbly, and he made me laugh. He told me that whatever happened to me in life, I would always be known as the girl who won *Big Brother*. I don't mind that one bit – if it wasn't for *Big Brother* I wouldn't be where I am now. I'm happy with that.

I spent the rest of the day back in Essex, showing the *Living the Dream* crew around my home town. It felt a bit weird – you know how it feels when you go on holiday for a couple of weeks, and then come back and everything is the same but it feels a bit different? I'd not had chance to see the town since I came out of *Big Brother*. As usual, there were lots of people coming up to talk to me. I showed the cameras where I had my sunbeds, and where I got my gel nails done. The salons were really pleased, it was great publicity for them.

I spent the night with Preston at his brother's, and left early the next morning to fly to Germany. Alex and his girlfriend Ari (short for Arabella) are great and they were really cool about me staying there. They've got plenty of room, and gradually more and more of my clothes were going there. Mum was delighted that it was all working out for me.

The driver picked me up at Alex's, and neither he nor I realised there must have been a photographer hidden somewhere nearby. The next day my picture was splashed all over the *Sun*, and the whole world knew that me and Preston were together. We'd planned to keep it quiet for a while, but in a way it was a relief when it was out in the open. We could relax and be honest about it.

The trip to Germany was horrible – the only bad thing among all the wonderful things that have happened to me since winning *Celebrity Big Brother*. I was invited to go into the German *Big Brother* as a surprise guest. The German *Big Brother* is very different from ours: it's like a little community, with a farm, and there's a 'hotel' for guests to stay in. The housemates stay in for about a year, so it's a completely different show.

I had a German lesson at the Goethe Institute before I went, which I didn't enjoy because it was like being back in a classroom at school. And I didn't learn any German, which didn't matter too much as most of the housemates could speak some English. I was supposed to go into it for two nights, but I wasn't at all happy, and I insisted on leaving after one.

I think it came too soon after my own time in *Celebrity Big Brother*. It just felt wrong being cut off from my normal life again, especially as my life had changed so much and was so exciting. I couldn't bear not being able to talk to Preston and to my mum. I wanted to cry. I was so lonely. If it hadn't been for the crew of *Living the Dream*, who were still following me, I don't know what I would have done.

When I went inside the 'hotel' I found there were cameras in the shower and the toilet. I didn't feel comfortable with that: we hadn't had cameras in there in *Celebrity Big Brother*, although I know they do in the normal *Big Brother* here. They promised me that they wouldn't be filming. I asked for a screen in the shower, but they didn't want to give me one. If they weren't planning to film, why couldn't I have a screen? The only time in the whole of the month that I was making the *Living the Dream* programmes that I asked the cameraman to stop filming was then: I was so upset and in tears, and I just didn't want to be seen like that on camera.

In the end they brought me a short screen, and the only time I had a shower I literally sat down on the floor of the shower. I was crying: my tears were running down my face with the shower water.

The German housemates were fine, and we tried to have a chat. But I didn't feel happy for one minute. I didn't want to be cut off again, I wanted to be out there enjoying my new life. I think if I was asked to do it now I would cope much better, but it was literally two weeks since I had come out of *Celebrity Big Brother* and I just wasn't ready to be isolated again. I still don't think I would enjoy it now, but I'd probably be better at putting up with it.

I kicked up so much fuss that I came out just twenty-six hours after I went in. I had to be quite firm – the German producers were trying to persuade me to stay. I said 'I'm really sorry, but I'm so unhappy.' Lucy, one of my friends from the *Living the Dream* team, was waiting for me, and I just fell into her arms when I came out. I flew home that evening. It was such a relief to be out of there.

It was so good to be home and to see Preston again. It really was difficult to spend time apart, especially as we had been used to being together twenty-four/seven in the house. We still hate it when we're not together.

I gained a day off by coming out of the German house early, but my two agents, Sally and Kat, took advantage of the extra time by having a meeting with me at their office. We had to discuss my upcoming schedule, what I would be doing over the next couple of weeks. I still found it hard to believe: there was me, sitting around a table with two top agents, working out if I had time to do all the work that was being offered to me. There were moments when I just sort of stood outside myself and thought: 'Weird, or what?'

The next day I had to do another roving reporter spot for *The Friday Night Project*. They'd loved the one the week before, where I rushed up to people and pretended to mistake them for celebs, so they asked me to do it again, this time at Brent Cross.

The researcher for the programme found the people. Sometimes I didn't have a clue who the celebrity was that they were supposed to look like – but then, that's not surprising as I didn't recognise most of the celebrities in the house.

I think the film crew were irritated by the number of people who just wanted to come up and talk to me. They wanted to get on with the filming and go home, but every time we tried to shoot something, someone would come up and ask for a picture with me, or just for a chat. When you've been in people's living room for three weeks they naturally think they know you.

The next few days are a blur of interviews, photo-shoots, and TV appearances. I did a good shoot for *Nuts* magazine, which was modelling underwear, and that evening I had to do two PAs (that's personal appearances), where I got paid just to turn up and say a few words at nightclubs. Both the nightclubs were near home in Essex, so I went back to Wickford to shower and change and grab something to eat. I was feeling guilty about Mum and Dean, as I was virtually living with Preston and I felt I didn't have enough time for them. But they were very understanding.

Mum just said: 'Enjoy it, you've got to do what you've got to do. We'll have time to catch up when your life isn't so hectic.'

And you can guess what Dean said: 'Live the dream, Chantelle, live the dream!'

The crowds in the nightclubs were great, all cheering me. I'd been in the Baker's Bar in Southend a few times before *Big Brother*, so it was while I was onstage there that I said, 'If any of the guys who have been talking about their affairs with me in the papers would like to come and introduce themselves, I'd love to meet you.'

I hadn't read what had appeared about me in the newspapers, but I knew that guys who had only seen me a couple of times had been giving interviews like they were the loves of my life. If you believed what it said in the papers, it would seem I'd had about ten serious boyfriends. Luckily, I could treat it all as a great big joke – I never got hurt by what was said in the press. None of my real friends talked about me, and they didn't treat me any differently from normal. But it was a bit of a wake-up call for me about what people will do for money.

I remember reading that Traci said I ignored her at the wrap party and that I have had a boob job. I didn't ignore anyone: it was so crowded and noisy it was hard to talk to people. And as for the boob job: if I've had one, I'd like my money back, please!

After the two PAs I got home to bed about 2.30 a.m., then I had to be up at 6 a.m. for an appearance on *Holly and Stephen's Saturday Showdown*, a kids' TV programme. I was beginning to feel run-down and ill. I had a bad sore throat – I think I had just been working too hard without any real time off. But I enjoyed the show: it was a laugh because they pretended to do a lie-detector test on me when they questioned me about Preston.

Preston was also very busy at this time. I remember the first time I went to see his band performing onstage in Nottingham: I could have burst with pride, watching him up there. I didn't know his music before I went in the house, but I'm now his biggest fan. I really love the songs. I know the other guys in the band now, and they're all great. They've made me feel very welcome.

I even stayed one night on the tour bus, but I didn't like sleeping in those little narrow bunk beds they have. I dreamed I was in a coffin, being buried alive. It was the combination of the small space and the air conditioning. I had to get up and sleep on a bench in the kitchen area. Preston woke up at 6.30 a.m. and couldn't see me in my bunk, and he thought I'd gone home or something. I don't think I fancy doing it again: I'm sure if you're with a band you get used to it, but I need my sleep.

My dad is also a big Ordinary Boys fan, he's got all their CDs. He's a real old mod, my dad, and like everyone else in the family, he loves Preston. Preston and I have a good laugh now and again about Kandy Floss (with a K!) and about the fact that people actually wanted me to record 'I Want It Right Now'. I hope I've gained a bit of respect by refusing to do it: it would have been so unfair to all the struggling musicians who deserve the breaks.

At about this time Preston went to the *NME* awards, and there were lots of photographers there hoping to get a picture of us together. But it was early days and we still wanted to be very private about our relationship, we didn't want a big public display. Also, I wanted him to get recognition for his work with the band, not for *Celebrity Big Brother*. The papers said I snubbed the event, but that just wasn't the case. Apart from anything else, I was tired and run-down, and I needed some rest.

I was still reeling with happiness. I said on the *Living the Dream* programme: 'I feel like that programme, *Goodnight Sweetheart*, when you go to the bottom of the garden and you step into another world. And it's a lovely world. I'm the happiest I've ever been.'

I still feel like that.

But me and Preston had to separate for a few days. He went to Japan with his band for five days – he's been there eight times in the last two years, and the band are really big out there. I also went abroad, to Marbella, for a dream of a job: I became a roving reporter for *GMTV* for a whole week. It was part of a giveaway competition they were running, and it was my job to show viewers what a life of luxury was all about, and what they could do if they won the daily prize of £10,000.

The first luxurious thing was a white stretch limo to pick me up at the airport, then my hotel suite. I had a jacuzzi on the roof! I was so excited when I saw it that I rang Mum, waking her up in the middle of the night. The next day I had to be up early to get in the stretch limo that took me to Puerto Banus. I'd only ever seen boats before at Canvey Island: now there were miles of huge luxury yachts. I got to go out in one, and they let me have a go steering it. It was such a giggle: I even posed on the bow like Kate Winslet in *Titanic*.

I was there for four days. I went up in a helicopter, which I didn't like at all because I kept thinking I was going to fall out. At one time I could swear the helicopter turned upside down. I know they can't do that but it felt like it – I left my tummy behind somewhere. The producer said afterwards that he lost count of how many times I said 'Oh my God!'

I was shown round a house which cost £4 million – can you believe that? But perhaps the best bit was doing a radio programme out there. The presenter talked about my dad, and they rang him on the show. I thought he might think it was a wind-up (he's had plenty!), so as soon as he picked up the phone I jumped in with 'Dad. Dad, it's me!' I didn't want him to swear and cut the call off! We had a quick chat and then he spoke to the presenter. He said lovely things about me.

'I'm very, very proud. She's a lovely girl and everyone is now finding out what I've known for years – that girl is a star!'

How nice is that? He's always been great about encouraging me and telling me how proud he is of me and Gregg.

I loved doing my reports for *GMTV*. I felt tired, because I was also filming *Living the Dream* at the same time, but as soon as the cameras pointed at me I found it easy to perform. I remember walking along the beach at Marbella, surrounded by all this flashy wealth, and thinking: 'Bloody hell! How did I get this lucky?'

The only difficult thing was not being able to talk to Preston. His mobile doesn't work in Japan – just as well, because you can imagine what the bill would have been! He managed to call me once, a really long phone call. It was strange not being in touch all the time, because even when we're apart we're always talking on the phone or texting each other. Luckily we were both busy, which kept our minds off not being together.

I was on the phone to Mum constantly. My phone bill for my first month out of the house was £600. I remembered how I could never pay it before, and it was always a terrible day when the bill dropped through the letter box. Now I could run it up and not worry – although I do know that I have got to be more careful, as it's silly to spend so much.

I do love spending money on clothes, but I'm not stupidly extravagant. As part of *Living the Dream*, I spent a day with a top stylist and designer, David Kappo, to get the low-down on how to improve my image. He took me clothes shopping at Harrods, but I nearly fainted when I saw the price tags on the clothes. I liked a little white vest top we saw – it was £1,130. David said it was worth every penny, but to me it was just a little bit of cloth, the kind of top you find dropped down the bottom of your wardrobe because you forgot about it. I can't believe anyone would pay that. The quality may be good, but it's a fashion item, you won't be wearing it in ten years' time.

Buying designer clothes seems ridiculous to me, especially if they are dresses you can only wear once to big events, where everyone sees them. However much money I ever have, I don't think I will be able to justify spending thousands of pounds of one dress.

The owner of Harrods, Mohammed Al Fayed, came by to see us while we were filming. I was a bit star-struck. He took us to the café and ordered a hot chocolate for me. Apparently he walks around Harrods every day, and I can imagine the staff all brushing themselves down and whispering, 'He's coming.' While we were there, I went to see the shrine to his son Dodi and Princess Diana: it was very moving. I felt so sorry for him, to have lost a son in such a tragic way.

David, the stylist, was really rude about my hair and make-up. He said my hair was 'brassy'.

'You could look more sophisticated, a little less Page Three. It looks a bit dolly-bird.'

I don't think I really gained anything from seeing him and I think he was wrong about my make-up: bright lipstick makes me happy. As for the clothes: I reckon I can find just as good on the high street for a fraction of the price.

Since *Living the Dream* was broadcast, so many people have stopped me in the street and said: 'Don't listen to that man! Your style is right for you.'

Doing the *Richard & Judy* show was great. Talking to them is just like having a chat in their living room. I felt I knew them, because I'd seen them so often, and they felt they knew me because of watching me in the house.

Before I did their show, I had a masterclass in television presenting, with Fiona Phillips from *GMTV*. I was thrilled when she said there wasn't much she could teach me. She'd seen the reports I'd done from Marbella, and she said I already did the right things, like using my hands to illustrate what I'm saying, so that I wasn't just a 'talking head' reading an autocue. If you watched me in the house, you'll know I always make lots of gestures with my hands – you'd have to tie them behind my back to stop me.

Fiona told me to always make sure I was comfortable with what I had to say. If the producer put words on the autocue which weren't the sort of words I would use, I should always ask for them to be changed. Then she threw me in at the deep end and made me interview her on camera. It was tricky, but I think I did quite well. The main tip she gave me for doing an interview is to always listen to what the other person says.

The *Living the Dream* team also arranged for me to meet the astrologer Russell Grant for a reading. I don't read horoscopes and I really don't know whether I believe in astrology. Russell told me I was a typical Leo:

'You are loving, adoring, so warm. You like to be loved, you like people to show you affection.' He also said I was a bubbly, happy person.

But I think anyone who had watched *Celebrity Big Brother* could have read my character just as well. What I find hard to believe with the horoscopes in magazines is that everyone from each star sign is supposed to have the same kind of day or week. It doesn't work like that.

Another thing I enjoyed doing was to go back on *Soccer AM*, only this time I wasn't just a 'Soccerette', I was a guest on the red sofa. Who would have guessed only five months ago when I first appeared, that I'd be back so soon, but in such a different way? It really brought it home to me how much my life had changed.

Afterwards, I went to see Nan and Grandad for the first time since Christmas. Preston came to meet them, and Mum and Dean were there, too – plus the film crew from *Living the Dream*, who were still following me everywhere!

Nan really like Preston – you can tell that by the fact she made an enormous pile of sandwiches for everyone. If she makes sandwiches, that's her seal of approval. They're really young in spirit, my grandparents, well funky. Preston took to them straight away. He already knew Mum and Dean, as we'd been out for a meal with them in London. As Mum said, they knew a lot more about him than most parents ever do about their daughter's boy-friends, as they'd been watching him on TV for three weeks. They already knew they liked him even before they met him.

I'd met Preston's dad, and his brother and sister, but not his mum as she lives in France – I only met her just before our wedding. All his family are lovely – it wasn't at all daunting meeting them for the first time – and they've made me feel very welcome. I chose his sister Lucy to be my only bridesmaid.

Preston bought this belly dancing outfit for me on our honeymoon in Morocco.

In front of the pool at our hotel.

Preston and I exploring the markets of Marrakesh.

Us in front of our hotel in Marrakesh.

It was so lovely to meet so many of my fans on my book tour.

At another book signing.

At the National
Television
Awards in
October 2006.

Us at a family
wedding.

Watching 2007's *Celebrity Big Brother* housemates from
the other side of the mirrors.

Finding time to see people was the biggest problem – with Dad from time to time I just had to grab half an hour sitting in his cab, chatting. Luckily, like Mum, he understood that it was difficult for me.

It was great to see my grandparents.

Grandad said: 'Didn't you do well?' To him I'm still the little girl who bit his table leg and used to trot down to the shops holding his hand to get chocolate.

We drove back to London that night, and the nicest thing ever was having the whole of the next day off together. I was very tired, and I hated being so tired because I wanted to be awake when I was with Preston.

We'd made plans to go off on holiday a few days later. We'd chosen Morocco because it was somewhere we'd never been, and it would be hot even in early March. But before we could go I had another couple of really busy days.

I did a lingerie shoot for Marks & Spencer, who were launching a new line of undies for younger women, called Ceriso. It was all very pretty and girlie, just my kind of stuff. I was thrilled when they let me keep some of it. I've always loved M&S, but it had always been too expensive for me. The photoshoot was for the *Daily Mail*, which made me feel very posh and upmarket. I'd never in my wildest dreams imagined I would be in the *Daily Mail* wearing M&S!

I'd acquired some more new knickers: Preston gave me some of the ones with Ordinary Boys written on them, which they sell at their gigs. It was an honour to wear them!

The shoot took all day, and the next day I had another one for Carphone Warehouse, for posters to launch their new pink Motorola Sliver phone, which was aimed at young girls. A poster of me was in the window of every Carphone Warehouse shop in the country. I also had to appear on *Loose Women*, which is a very lively lunchtime chat show with some very feisty women. The presenter, Carol McGiffin, said about me: 'She's not stupid, but she's a little bit blonde.' It would have been easy to feel overpowered by all those talkative women, but I think I held my own.

Afterwards I said on camera for *Living the Dream*: 'Obviously I'm getting paid, but to get paid for something you love doing is bloody goddamned bloody wicked!'

I still feel exactly like that. I love walking down the street and being recognised. Only the other day, a little boy of about five shouted out 'Dad, Dad, there's Chantelle from *Big Brother*!' and just afterwards I had a lady of about seventy telling me she had voted for me to win. I've been really lucky, most people have been very nice to me.

I'd love to take every teenage girl on the journey with me. I'd love to share it with everyone. I'll never forget any of it. This is what I've wanted all my life, what I've been building up for. I feel I've been living this life in my imagination for five years or more, and that's why I'm not overawed by it. This is what my life was meant to be. It's unbelievable, but everything has come out right for me. Completely. Wicked, or what?

Chapter Fifteen

Will You Marry Me?

After our holiday in Morocco, I moved in properly with Preston. He lives in Brighton, in a flat he bought only a couple of months before he went into *Celebrity Big Brother*. He was brought up in the area, and I love it too, so we plan in the near future to buy ourselves a house not too far away. We've been house-hunting, but what with all the wedding arrangements, there hasn't been much time. It's our next big project.

But hang on – I'm getting ahead of myself. I haven't even told you about the engagement yet . . .

The trip to Morocco was only a four-day break: there simply wasn't time to get away for longer. We'd had to compare diaries to even find that much free time. But it was just what we needed, a chance to be completely alone together. I was still filming *Living the Dream*, and at first there was a plan for the crew to come with us. But I think they could see we needed a bit of time off, so they gave us a video camera and asked us to film ourselves, which added to the fun. It also gave a nice 'home movie' feel to that bit of the programme when it was broadcast.

We stayed in a very secluded hotel, recommended by Alex, Preston's brother. Mostly we just chilled, but we also explored the markets, went on a trip to the Atlas Mountains, bathed in a waterfall and found nice restaurants for cosy meals. We even rode a camel, which looks great on the video – luckily, we don't have 'smellyvision' or you would know what a real stinker our camel was!

It was a wonderful time for both of us, away from all the pressures of work and all the press coverage that surrounded us back in Britain. It is so easy being with Preston: we've never had any rows, although he'll tell you that I pout a bit when I don't get my own way! Seriously, we discovered in the *BB* house that we got along together as friends first, before we had a romance. That's a great way to start a relationship, because we really knew each other after twenty-three days, all the good bits and the bad bits, and we fell in love with the complete person. As Preston says, we packed about three years' worth of getting to know each other into three weeks. I recommend all young couples spend three weeks together in *Big Brother* – they'd certainly know at the end of it whether they're meant to be together! For the first time in my life, I am with someone I trust completely.

As soon as we flew back to England, the madness started again. The same day that we landed at Heathrow, I was back at the airport flying out to Greece for an *OK!* magazine fashion shoot. I didn't have time to go home. I went into London, spent a couple of hours with my agent and then it was off to Heathrow again. I carried the same suitcase, complete with the dirty clothes from Morocco. As ever, I'd packed loads of things, so I had plenty of clean stuff as well. I did leave some of the bags I bought in Morocco (loads!) at my agent's office.

The shoot was in northern Greece, at Halkidiki, and I was away for three days. It looks lovely in the pictures in the magazine – and it *was* lovely. The only problem was that it was early March, and freezing. It was as cold as Britain, though at least it didn't rain. But posing for bikini shots and looking relaxed at the same time took all my modelling skills, as between shots I was shivering with four layers of clothing on. My muscles seized up at one point.

On the way back to the airport I was on the phone the whole way, doing the interview which would go with the pictures. I was becoming a really experienced interviewee, and it was much easier now that everything with Preston was in the open. I didn't have to use any tricks to turn the questions round on the interviewer.

There were loads more TV appearances and magazine interviews to do. I was on *Eight Out of Ten Cats* with Jimmy Carr. Most of the other panellists were comedians, and half the time I didn't know what they were going on about. Once I even forgot who we were discussing. I was sure Jimmy wouldn't come back to me but he said, 'What do you think Chantelle?' and I had to admit I didn't know what we were talking about. Never mind, it played up to my dumb-blonde image. I've seen Jimmy a couple of times since, and he's been lovely.

I also did the *Drivetime* show on Capital with Richard Bacon. I prefer TV to radio, although I must admit radio is a lot easier – you don't have to worry about your make-up or your hair.

Now magazine came up with a great idea for a spread: they asked Jade to interview me. Jade Goody is one of the only people to have done really well out of being in *Big Brother*, and I really admire her. I'd met her briefly, just to say hello, but this was the first time we had sat down together for a proper chat. She was lovely, funny and chatty. We were bouncing off each other: we had such a lot in common, because we'd both been dismissed as the dumb ones in the house. I liked her immediately, and I think she liked me.

I did a photoshoot to launch my new column in *More* magazine. It's an agony aunt column: they send me three or four problems that readers have written in with each week, and I give my advice. They are the sorts of problems young girls have: boyfriends, bitchiness from other girls, that kind of thing. I think what I would do if it was me in that situation, or what would I tell a good friend if it was her. (I have another column, testing cosmetics and beauty products for *New* magazine, and during the summer I also wrote a column for *OK!* about *Big Brother*.)

The funny thing was that on the day I was doing the *More* shoot, Duncan from Blue was at the same studio. It was really weird, because I used to buy his albums. I can remember when I was about thirteen, me and my mates used to pretend that Blue were singing just to us, and now here I was chatting to him

I filmed a sketch for the last ever *Top of the Pops Reloaded*, with Sam and Mark. It was about a pop agency that was losing money. I was the secretary, and then I released a huge-selling record and saved the agency. It was great fun – I enjoy acting. I think I've proved I can do it, after four days pretending to be in Kandy Floss!

Another job I did was very close to my heart. I did a photoshoot and interview to help launch the Bully Watch London campaign. We released 130 balloons, each one representing a thousand children involved with bullying in London every day.

I talked about my own experiences. I want all those kids to know that you can feel as though you are on the floor, but you can come back, and be where I am now. It may not seem like it at the time, but it makes you stronger. I want kids to have the courage to get the help they need. They are not alone, there are organisations like beatbullying they can turn to. I think it helps a great deal if you realise there are others with the same problem.

I was able to squeeze a few days off, which was great, because I needed a chance to rest and go shopping for clothes before the next round of filming began: I was about to make my own TV series – how exciting is that? Endemol came up with the idea of *Chantelle's Dream Dates*, which we described as 'a quest to rescue the dateless'. The idea was that I would find a member of the public who was single, and in the space of one day I would find three possible dates for them to choose from. I loved having my own show. It was broadcast on E4 but has been repeated on Channel 4, and I'm really proud of it.

But before filming started I had another official duty: I presented one of the awards at the British Book Awards, hosted by Richard and Judy. It was at the Dorchester Hotel, and there were lots of stars there: Jimmy Carr and Jamie Oliver both said hello to me. I presented the award to the best newcomer, Monica Lewycka, who wrote *A Short History of Tractors in Ukrainian*. I haven't read it, and the title definitely puts me off, but I'm told it's a very funny book. I just wish she'd had an easier name – whenever I have to present something, it seems the winners have difficult names.

Making *Chantelle's Dream Dates* was great because I was working with my friends Jo, Becks and Lucy again. It was very hard work, starting at 7 a.m. and often not finishing until 10 p.m. Each episode took three days to make, and we were working non-stop for five weeks. The whole of April passed in a blur as far as work was concerned.

But as far as my private life was concerned, it was the most fantastic month ever. Yes, this is when Preston proposed to me.

It was on 10 April, two months after we officially got together. I'd had a long, tiring day filming, and I'd travelled back to Brighton, not getting home until about 8.30 p.m. It was lovely to be home, as Preston wasn't working that evening, and so we could just cuddle up together on the sofa. I always treasure the times when we are on our own, with nothing special to do. We love staying home together, sharing the cooking, which we both enjoy. We watch films on TV, and have a bottle of wine. When you are with someone you love, even normal things like shopping for food become exciting, because you are doing them together.

But this night turned out to be very special. Preston's mother and father are divorced, and his mother lives in France. I knew that he had asked her to send over a very special ring. It's a family heirloom, which dates back in Preston's father's family for several generations, when it was given as an engagement ring to his great-grandmother. Preston is descended from Earl Grey, who is famous for the brand of tea named after him, and his great-grandmother was Sybil Grey.

When it arrived from France I saw it, and I suppose I had an inkling why he wanted it, but I didn't want to assume anything. Anyway, we were chatting about our future together, telling each other how happy we are and how much we love each other, when Preston said:

'Hold on a minute,'

He went through to the bedroom and returned with the ring, then he held my hand.

'Chantelle, will you marry me?' he said.

I replied without any hesitation: 'Of course I will.' I couldn't think of anything I wanted more, and I was so happy I felt I would burst.

Preston took me in his arms and kissed me, then we danced around the bedroom singing 'We're going to the chapel and we're gonna get married' and the Ramones song 'Baby, I Love You'. I was so excited it's a wonder I didn't spontaneously combust.

Then we wandered down the hill hand in hand to the off-licence to buy champagne. It was absolutely lovely, the best evening ever. I never knew that something could feel this good. I hit the phone to share the news with Mum, Dad and everybody else. Gregg texted me that he loved me and was so proud of me.

Just a few months before I didn't think I ever wanted to be married. I'd have said a massive 'NO' to marriage and kids. But meeting Preston completely changed all that. We both want to have babies one day, although we'll put it off for a little while because we are both so busy. But I'd really love to have Preston's children.

It was a beautifully romantic night, and the ring slipped on to my finger easily. It is the most lovely ring ever, with six diamonds, very pretty and just perfect. I loved it instantly, and it's so nice that there is all that history behind it. It was lovely that he felt he could give it to me, and I'm honoured to wear it. I didn't want to ever take it off.

But a couple of days later I realised I *couldn't* take it off. Preston put cream all over my finger and eventually, after a lot of struggle, we managed to get it off. But then we couldn't get it back on: my finger was really swollen.

It was the evening, which meant we couldn't take it anywhere, so I had to go to work the next day, filming *Dream Dates*, without it. I sat on the train from Brighton to London trying to get it on, but it just wouldn't go. I was distraught. I didn't want anyone to notice that I hadn't got it, because it would look as if I wasn't wearing Preston's ring – I'd been showing it off to everybody. But more important, I just wanted to have it on, to be engaged to Preston.

When we were filming that day I borrowed some gloves from one of the directors. It wasn't even a really cold day, and these were great big biker-type gloves in padded leather: they didn't exactly go with my white-and-grey jacket. In fact, they looked ridiculous, and probably drew more attention than if I'd just not worried about showing my ringless finger.

When we took the ring to a jeweller's, it turned out it was three and a half sizes too small, so how I got it on that evening when Preston proposed I don't know. I like to think it's an omen, like in a fairy story, and it means we will be happy ever after.

While the ring was being made bigger, Preston bought me a temporary one, gold with six diamonds in a row. He bought it in a pawn shop, and it's horrible to think that someone was so poor they had to pawn it, or maybe the girl said no to the proposal. I wore it for a couple of days, until my real ring was ready.

Another lovely thing that happened at about this time (although nowhere near as nice as getting engaged to Preston) was that Vauxhall lent me a brand new Tigra to use for six months. It's a pretty little car in a lovely pale blue colour. I can't drive yet, but I'm determined to. It's a great thrill: I wanted to learn to drive before, and I had even passed my theory test and had a few lessons. But I didn't have enough money to carry on. The irony is that now I've got the car and can have the lessons, the most difficult thing is to find time. I've started learning with Dad, who has shown me the basics. I bounced the car up and down a bit discovering how to use the gears – it's like having to have a brain in your feet. But now I've got the hang of that, Dad says my main problem is driving too fast for a learner. He's very patient with me, thankfully.

Mum has also been brave enough to go out with me with my L-plates on. The other day I was driving along with her and I went from second to fifth gear instead of to third. The car juddered a bit and stalled, and the man behind nearly ran into the back of us. I sometimes wonder if I will ever be good enough to pass my test. Then I remember my friend Nicole – if she can do it, so can I. We all tease her about her driving. I was in the car with her once when she had a run-in with a petrol tanker on a garage forecourt. Luckily nobody was hurt. It was such a ridiculous thing to happen I just fell about laughing, and so did she.

My other grandmother, Dad's mum, died at this time – his dad had died a few years earlier. It was a very sad time for Dad. I never knew his parents as well as I know Mum's, because they lived in London so I didn't see them as much. But I know how upset he was, and I made sure I was there for him. He says that I was a real help and support. I think my driving lessons helped to take his mind off it – teaching me to drive requires full concentration! I persuaded him one day to drive me into London, and I took him for tea at Harrods, to cheer him up.

I was exhausted when we finished filming *Dream Dates* in the first week of May. I don't think I managed to set up any great romances with my matchmaking, although one couple definitely clicked and did go out together a few times. But I think they all had fun, and enjoyed the experience.

The day after we finished making the series, I was on camera again for two different programmes: I was interviewed for a programme called *Big Brother: The Relationships*. I was asked what I thought about relationships in the house, and there were a few questions about Preston, inevitably. Then I was whisked away by car to record a *Celebrity Weakest Link*, with loads of other reality TV stars. It was all for charity, so I was happy to do it, but I think because I had been working non-stop I was very tired and had a terrible headache.

The other guests were Russell Grant, who had done *Celebrity Fit Club*; Jo from *The Apprentice*; MC Plat'num from Blazin Squad who did *The Games*; Jilly Goolden, the wine expert, who was on *I'm a Celebrity, Get Me Out of Here*; ex-footballer Mick Quinn, who was also on *Celebrity Fit Club*, and a couple called the Armstrongs who had a reality series made about their business. From *Celebrity Big Brother*, Maggot and Michael Barrymore were there. I was glad it was those two, as they were my friends in the house, and I just wasn't feeling up to meeting some of the others, like George or Dennis. I really wasn't feeling at all well, but it was still lovely to meet those two again.

I psyched myself up to cope with Anne Robinson, who made a few cracks about me being a blonde bimbo and a 'bottle blonde'. I didn't do too badly – I didn't go out until round four, and I was actually the strongest link in one round. All I cared about was not being the first to go. It truly was a petrifying experience.

I was feeling really ill, so I was grateful to be voted off. The bright lights were making my head ache, my lips were beginning to swell and my eyes were becoming puffy. I think I was just exhausted: it had been a punishing work schedule.

The other contestants were all lovely.

When Mick nominated me he said: 'I'll get a kick when I get home, because we love Chantelle.'

When she told me I was going, I said to Anne: 'Please don't be horrible to me. I don't like it.'

She said: 'I think you've done terrifically well, and it's been lovely having you here.'

When it was shown, it didn't seem as if she was nasty to me at all. But on the night she was a bit rotten to me, as she is to everyone. They edited the worst of it out, in my case.

A few weeks ago I was sitting at the hairdresser's when a woman came up behind me and looked in the mirror and smiled. I smiled back, thinking it was just someone being nice. Then she whispered in my ear: 'You don't know who I am, do you?'

I turned round, and it was Anne. She was really lovely, so different from the personality she adopts for the show. I told her that she scared me. But she said something really nice:

'Your mum and dad are probably really proud of you – they should be.'

The next photoshoot I did for *OK!* was great fun, because

Preston was there. It was the first time we had done anything together, and we had a laugh. We each had our own stylist, and different rooms to dress in. It was the first time we'd done an interview together, but we both felt very comfortable with it.

The stylists always bring more clothes than they need, and occasionally there will be something that just isn't me, so I don't wear it. But one thing I have learned is that you can't judge until you have tried it on. Some things look so much better on the hanger than they do on, and others, which look nothing hanging up, are amazing when you wear them.

When I go shopping for clothes now, I'm more prepared to try things on before I decide they're not right. I was shopping with Mum recently and I really didn't think much of a dress, but I took it with me into the changing room and after I saw it on, I bought it immediately.

I'm so not a party girl: Preston and I spend our evenings just chilling, maybe going out for a meal or to see friends. We don't go to nightclubs to meet other celebrities. So it's ironic that when I did get a party invite – to the tenth birthday bash for *OK!* – it was on the same night as the wrap party for *Chantelle's Dream Dates*. Imagine: two parties in one evening! I felt like a real celebrity. I wore a green floral dress which I'd bought in Top Shop – very colourful, and every bit as nice as an expensive designer number.

I went early to the *OK!* one, which was very glamorous and full of famous people like Lulu and Melinda Messenger. Preston was busy that night, so he couldn't come with me. The owner of *OK!*, Richard Desmond, came over to thank me for appearing in the magazine. I said, 'No – thank *you*,' which is exactly what I said to Phil and Sharon when they thanked me for being in *Celebrity Big Brother*. Imagine these people wanting to thank me – I'm grateful to them for all the opportunities I have had.

The wrap party was fun, because I was with all my friends from Endemol. We watched the last episode on a big screen.

One of the most exciting things of all that has happened to me in this amazing year, is meeting Prince Charles. I was invited to a reception for his charity, the Prince's Trust, at his London home, Clarence House. I'd no idea what to wear. It was from 5 p.m. to 7.30 p.m., so I didn't want to look too dressy. In the end I settled on black trousers and a black top from Miss Sixty, with a belt, shoes and bag which all matched, from Dune. I felt comfortable and smart.

It was a spectacular event, with loads of famous people there like Sharon and Ozzy Osbourne, Cat Deeley, Phillip Schofield, Kate Thornton, the Bee Gees. I felt a bit guilty being lucky enough to get an invite, as I knew lots of people would have loved to be there. I kept thinking: 'What am I doing here?' Mum was so impressed when she heard I was going: 'God, can you believe it?' she kept saying. I don't think I realised until I got there just how special it was.

It was weird walking in. It's like a normal house, only bigger and posher. There are school photos of Prince William and Prince Harry, and that reminds you that it is a home, not just an official residence. I didn't know anyone, so it would have been nice if I could have taken someone with me. Lots of people came up and spoke to me but I was worried that I'd end up standing on my own. There were waitresses taking champagne and little nibbles of food around.

Prince Charles came into the room and spoke to everyone individually. When he began talking to the girl next to me I knew it was my turn next, and I was quite nervous. Just as he turned towards me he stopped and turned back to say something else, which added to the tension. He was with Ant and Dec, and Dec told him who I was and introduced me. I'd never met Dec before, but he was very kind and really helped me out. Prince Charles obviously hadn't a clue who I was.

'How extraordinary. You were locked up in a house for three weeks?' he said, after Dec explained.

He asked me what I had planned for later in the year, and I told him I was getting married.

'What, to someone else from the house?' he said.

'Yeah,' I replied.

Although his voice is very posh, he was much more relaxed and normal than I expected. I liked Princess Diana and always wondered what she saw in him. But now I have met him I can see it. He has a sense of humour, and he's quite rugged-looking in a posh sort of way.

My picture, talking to him, was in the papers the next day. One of them put the headline 'CHAS MEETS CHAV' on it. I don't care, although I'm definitely *not* a chav. As far as I'm concerned, it's just another lovely picture to add to the huge pile of newspaper cuttings that Mum keeps in boxes.

The work I did to support the Prince's Trust was to appear on a celebrity version of *Blankety Blank*. I was on with Stephen Fry, but I'd no idea before the programme who he was. He beat me, but I answered the question in a jokey way instead of seriously. Ronnie Corbett was one of the celebrities on the panel, and he came up to me after the show and asked me if I'd lost weight, because he thought I looked a bit skinny. It was one of those amazing moments, realising that Ronnie Corbett, who I used to watch on telly when I was a little kid, knew who I was.

Jonathan Ross was also on the panel, and I met him again when I appeared on his chat show with Preston. It's quite a coup, to be invited on to his show, and it was great doing it with Preston. Jonathan is famous for giving some of his guests a hard time, but he was fine with us. Jon Bon Jovi and Noel Edmonds were also on the programme, and we had a nice little chat with Noel.

Another fun event was appearing on the big Sport Relief fund-raiser. Jade Goody and I competed against each other at *Mastermind*, with that big black chair, the spotlight and John Humphrys. My specialist subject was *Coronation Street*, which I always watch, and Jade's was *EastEnders*. She beat me on that round, but I managed to do better in the general knowledge, so I was the overall winner. Not that we cared who won: we were both thrilled to do something to help. And it was great meeting Jade again, we had a good laugh.

But by far the most exciting thing I was doing at this time was planning the wedding. We both wanted to get married as soon as we could. We didn't want a really long engagement: we had decided to get married and we wanted to get on with it. August was the right choice: we wanted good weather and it was only a few days after my twenty-third birthday.

There was such a lot to do before I could become Mrs Chantelle Preston . . .

Chapter Sixteen

The Best Day of My Life

Mrs Chantelle Preston. How nice is that? Mrs Chantelle Preston, I keep saying it to myself, because it sounds so lovely. I've also had to learn a new signature. It's all completely exciting.

Preston is actually called Samuel Preston, and his friends all call him Sam. But because Preston is the name he uses with the band, that's the name he was introduced to me by, so I find it hard to think of him as Sam, although I do use it sometimes. But it's really lovely me being Mrs Preston: it makes me feel very close to him.

My wedding day was the best day of my life. I know people always say that, but it really was. I didn't think anything would ever beat winning *Celebrity Big Brother*, but this was in a different class. It was really, really special.

We didn't have a lot of time to plan the wedding – not compared with how long lots of couples take. But we both felt very strongly that we weren't engaged to be engaged, we were engaged to be married. We didn't want a long engagement, we wanted to be married. I think that when you meet the right person, you just know. We could have lived together for three years and it wouldn't have made any difference, we'd still be perfect for each other. So there was no point in waiting.

Also, I think Preston summed it up when he said that three weeks in the Big Brother house, seeing each other all the time, is the equivalent of being together for a year in the normal world. It's such an intense time, you get to know the best and the worst in people.

Planning the wedding was really exciting. At times it was a bit frantic, but I don't mind that. I'm always a last-minute person, and I thrive on it. We were both so busy we found it really hard making time to organise everything. We decided on August from the moment we got engaged, because it's a lovely month, with a very good chance of nice weather. (And it's also my birthday month – I was twenty-three four days before the wedding.)

One of the first things I did in preparation was get myself toned up. One of the magazines took a really terrible snatched picture of me and wrote about my 'jelly belly', and one journalist even suggested I was pregnant. So even though I'm quite slim, I decided that I did need to tone my figure.

I started working out with a personal trainer called Sharon. She really put me through my paces at the gym, and gave me exercises to do at home using an exercise ball. She would text me every day to make sure I was doing them. I stuck at it pretty well, except for the final week before the wedding when I was just too busy. I'm really pleased with the results, and I've been told I look slimmer, even though that's not what I was trying to achieve. I just feel that I'm more toned.

Finding a venue for the wedding was tricky, because we didn't have lots of time to look for one. We eventually decided to spend a whole day touring London – where we both wanted to get married – looking at five or six different places. We'd heard about Dartmouth House, and we'd been told 'When you see it, you'll know it's right'. And that's just what happened: we walked in and looked at each other and we were both feeling the same thing. It was perfect. An added attraction was that it had an enclosed courtyard, so we could go outside if the weather was good. We decided to have a gazebo erected in the courtyard so that we could hold the service out there.

Dartmouth House is a really lovely old mansion, very traditional, with huge marble fireplaces, wood-panelled walls and painted ceilings. There's a beautiful staircase, just perfect for a bride to make her entrance.

Me and Preston had exactly the same ideas about what our wedding should be like. We wanted it to be very traditional, very old-fashioned, and we definitely wanted a small wedding: neither of us would have felt comfortable with lots of people we hardly knew there. We just wanted close family and friends.

It was a really special day for me when Elizabeth Emanuel, who, with her then husband David, designed Princess Diana's wedding dress, offered to make my dress for me. I couldn't have been more excited. It took at least eight fittings to get it just perfect. Elizabeth interpreted what I wanted exactly: the dress was everything I dreamed it should be. Again, I knew I didn't want anything modern and I didn't want anything twinkly or sparkly. I wanted traditional elegance, and that's exactly how it worked out. It was made in a beautiful ivory satin, a corset bodice which left my shoulders and arms bare, and a big ruched skirt. Every time I went for a fitting I felt just a little bit more excited as it started to take shape.

I decided early on that I only wanted one bridesmaid – Preston's sister Lucy. Again, it was part of my idea to keep everything simple.

Elizabeth made Lucy's dress, which was very similar in style to mine but simpler and in a beautiful deep red-rose colour, to match the wedding flowers.

It looked stunning with her really dark hair. We had everywhere decorated with red roses, and I carried a traditional large shower bouquet of blood-red roses, which looked amazing against my ivory dress. I associate roses with a very English, classical look, which was exactly what I wanted.

Elizabeth also made a dress for my mum. I wanted all the women at the wedding to wear long dresses, because I felt that would complete the old-fashioned, traditional theme. We arranged the wedding for four o'clock in the afternoon, so that long dresses wouldn't look too out of place during the day. Mum's dress was really lovely, in a pale gold fabric that suited her perfectly. It was sleeveless, with a basque bodice and a shawl collar which just touched her shoulders. She looked really fantastic.

Everyone had new clothes. Mum made sure Dean had a new suit, and Dad bought himself one too at the very last minute. I think he got it two days before the big day. I obviously take after him because I always leave everything to the last possible chance. The men wore dark suits with white shirts and deep red ties to match the flowers.

Nan and Grandad also had new outfits. Nan loved her long dress with a big, pale pink hat. Even my great-gran, who is 102, was able to make it to the ceremony, which was really fantastic. She lives with my auntie. It was very special having my photo taken with her – there were four generations of us there.

I chose the long-dress theme because I had a vision of it looking like the ballroom scene from *The Sound of Music*, one of my favourite childhood films, and it did. The setting was perfect, and all the colourful dresses looked gorgeous.

But I'm getting ahead of myself – I've still got more to tell you about the wedding preparations.

My hen party was a couple of weeks before the big day. Eighteen of us, including my mum, went to a nightclub in London called Sugar Reef. The girls had hired a stretch excursion – it's like a stretch limo but it looks like a jeep. We had a really really good night. I can't tell you what we got up to because I had a few drinks and I honestly don't remember it. If I did remember it, it would probably mean I hadn't had such a good time! I do remember getting home long past my bedtime!

Preston went out for a stag night with his friends in Brighton, but he also had five days in Mali, in Africa, with his brother Alex and his two best friends.

The week before the wedding was very hectic. The previous weekend Preston's band were onstage at the massive V Festival, which was bigger than ever because there was no Glastonbury Festival. They appeared on Saturday at the V Festival site in Chelmsford, Essex, and the next day at the site in Weston Park, Staffordshire. I went with the band and, thankfully, this time they had a tour bus with a double bed in a closed-off area, so it wasn't uncomfortable like the first time I travelled with them, when I couldn't sleep on the narrow beds. I really enjoyed myself. The other lads in the band are great to be around, and despite it pouring with rain, it was a really good weekend.

It was my birthday on the Monday, and because we didn't think we'd be back until late, Preston gave me my present on the Friday. I had no idea what he had bought me, and I was bowled over by a beautiful pair of diamond stud earrings. They were the only jewellery I wore on my wedding day apart from my rings. I didn't want anything to detract from them or my dress, and they were just perfect.

For the same reason, on my wedding day I didn't wear anything on my head. I felt that a sparkly tiara would look completely wrong and would have defeated what the dress was all about.

Preston and I celebrated my birthday with a trip to the theatre in Covent Garden. We went to see *Blue Man Group*, which is a bizarre but very entertaining show staged by three men who are painted blue. There are songs, dancing, comedy, strobe lighting effects: it's hard to explain, but it was great fun and even a little bit scary at times. I really enjoyed myself.

The last three days before the wedding should have been packed with final preparations. I intended to spend one of the days shopping for bits and pieces for the honeymoon, but I came down with a really bad throat infection. I couldn't believe it: it was the week of my wedding and I was feeling really rotten, feverish and unwell, with a sore throat. I was feeling so bad I was crying. Preston looked after me and tried to cheer me up, but I was so worried that I wouldn't be well for the wedding. There was nothing for it but to stay at home and take a course of antibiotics, which I was still on by the big day. You're not really supposed to drink when you take antibiotics, but I broke the rules: imagine not being able to have a glass of champagne at your own wedding! Anyway, by then I was beginning to feel better, thank goodness.

But being poorly meant I didn't have time to get all the things I needed for our honeymoon. We decided to go to Morocco again, where we had had our very first holiday together. This time we went for complete luxury: we stayed in a hotel that had separate little villas, each with its own private swimming pool and its own butler. How posh is that? But we felt we deserved it, because we had both been so busy, and we'd had so little time to ourselves. As it was, we could only spend a week there because of other commitments. We didn't fly out until the Sunday after our Friday wedding.

Preston's band is so hectic that they were even performing on the Saturday night, the day after the wedding!

Knowing that it was going to be very hot in Morocco, I wanted to buy new bikinis, kaftans and summer dresses. Luckily, we have a friend, Luke, who is a stylist, and who understands what I like and what suits me. He very kindly went shopping for me, and brought a selection of clothes to the Chesterfield Hotel, which is next door to Dartmouth House, and where we stayed before and after the wedding. That was another reason for choosing Dartmouth House – the hotel has an exclusive access into the venue, so we could go straight from there into the wedding. I didn't want to go outside in my dress: I wanted it to look perfect and I was afraid of doing anything that might damage it. We had also arranged for the wedding to be covered exclusively in *OK!*, and there were lots of paparazzi lurking around outside and we were determined not to give them any chance of a picture.

There had even been paparazzi outside my hairdresser's, where I spent nine hours (don't laugh!) the day before the wedding. Richard Ward, whose salon is just off Sloane Square, has more or less been doing my hair since I came out of the house. He has lots of starry clients, and he does a lot of TV work himself. But that's not why I go there. I discovered his salon when we were filming *Dream Dates*, and when I found out they did extensions I went in. Richard and all his staff are really good, and I always come out feeling great.

But having my extensions done is a long job. I got there at 9 a.m. and didn't leave until 6 p.m.! All my extensions were removed, then my hair was coloured and then new extensions were put in.

My hair was the big surprise of the day for everyone – even me – as I literally only decided the day before that I was going to go dark brown.

That's my natural hair colour, and I've been thinking for a while of going back to it. I'd already been having some brown extensions mixed in with the blonde ones, but I felt that to go dark brown would be right with my dress.

I know most girls decide well in advance that they want to change their hair colour – well, like I say, I thrive on doing things at the last minute!

To fool the photographers, before I left the salon one of the girls popped out and bought a large cap. All my brown hair was pinned up, and then some blonde extensions were added all round to make it look like I'd still got my trademark blonde extensions.

I had hoped to do a bit of shopping before going to the hotel, but I was being pursued by so many photographers – there were about ten of them waiting for me – that I went straight to the hotel. Mum and Dean were there already, and we spent all evening in my room chatting. Mum popped out to buy some magazines, and we just chilled, drinking wine and eating Pringles. I saw Preston for about twenty minutes that night, but then we didn't meet again until the wedding. He loved my new hair colour. He went out to Nobu with some of his friends for a drink, and then stayed up chatting with his mum till the small hours in the hotel bar. It was weird knowing he was only two doors down the corridor.

I was able to go to sleep, but I woke up at four in the morning because I was so excited. I finally drifted off to sleep again but this time I woke from a nightmare in which I found that my wedding dress had been hacked and was too short!. It was only 7 a.m, but I couldn't get back to sleep.

I don't know where the day went. The wedding was not until four o'clock, and I had all day to pamper myself, but somehow the time flew by.

Richard, the hairdresser, came to the hotel to do my hair for me. He made it wavy, and I wore it loose.

Elizabeth Emanuel also came, with my dress. She had to struggle through the paparazzi and the reporters outside, and one of then tried to pull the cover off the dress to see what it looked like.

I also booked my favourite make-up artist, Joanna, who I met when I did previous shoots for *OK!* She's really nice, and she does my face exactly the way I like it, because she understands how I want to look.

She also did Lucy, Mum and Preston's mum, who flew in from her home in France the week of the wedding. It was the first time I'd met his mum because she lives abroad. It was great fun all of us getting ready together. We were all quite giggly – it was a typically girlie scene as you can probably imagine. I kept repeating how excited I was to be getting married.

My mum says she felt really emotional, so before the service began she went into the toilets and had a little cry. She told herself to get it over with, because she didn't want to be upset during the service.

I know it's fashionable for brides to be late, but I really didn't intend to be. But then at the last minute everyone was fussing over me – Richard, Joanna, Elizabeth – doing final bits and pieces, and I didn't get there until twenty past four.

Dad gave me away, and we went down the wonderful staircase together, with Lucy in front. Red roses had been strewn everywhere. When he took my arm Dad told me how much he loved me and how proud he was of me. He said I looked stunning. As we walked down together I felt so emotional I wanted to burst into tears, but I was desperate not to spoil my make-up. It was such a beautiful moment in time. We were getting married in the gazebo, in front of a beautiful fountain which was banked up with red roses. As I walked up the aisle, the Ramones' 'Baby I Love You' was playing – it's our song, the one Preston and I danced around the flat to on the day we were engaged. I was smiling broadly as I walked up, and all I can remember is a sea of faces all around me, all smiling back. Although I felt a bit nervous when Dad first arrived to take me down to the ceremony, as soon as I caught sight of Preston, I suddenly felt very calm.

There were sixty-eight guests altogether, so it was the small intimate wedding that we wanted, but with enough people to make it feel like a really big occasion. I spotted Mum at the very front, looking lovely. She told me later that she felt I looked like a princess and I thought the same about her. She looked really special.

Preston saw my dress for the first time as I walked up. He said later it took his breath away. I knew what he was going to wear: a black suit with one satin lapel, and a satin strip down the trousers, and white stitching round one pocket. He had a black cummerbund, a white shirt and a black tie. He looked even more gorgeous than usual.

He didn't say anything when I got alongside him but he gave me a wink and cheekily pointed to his watch to show how long I'd made him wait! It was a very simple ceremony, without any hymns. We both agreed that we wanted it to be very straightforward. I tried to keep my voice from shaking as I said my vows. When we got to the bit where I agreed to be Preston's wife Preston naughtily whispered, 'Yes!' making everyone in the room laugh. Then when Father Hicks said, 'You may now kiss the bride,' Preston took me by surprise by bending me right back in a long kiss like something out of a Hollywood musical. It was wonderful, really romantic. And the whole of the congregation clapped and cheered.

We'd had our rings made by a lovely jeweller's in Brighton, Grains of Gold. Preston had a plain gold band with the engraving 'Baby I Love You' around the inside. Mine is exquisite, cut to fit around my engagement ring. It is studded with diamonds and looks very pretty and Victorian, just perfect with the engagement ring. (For about a week before the wedding I wore the replacement ring we bought at the beginning, because I was nervous about anything happening to the real engagement ring.)

Mum says she was really glad that she could only see the back of my head during the service, because she was sitting behind me on the bride's side. She says if she had seen me it would probably have been too much, and she'd have cried again. As it was, she had to force herself to think of other things. But her eyes were full of tears, and she reckons lots of other people's were, too. My hair was a great surprise, of course, and afterwards so many people told me how much it suited me that I knew I made the right decision. Preston loved it too.

After the ceremony we had a pianist playing classical music as everyone went through and mingled while rosé champagne and cocktails were served.

We decided it would be a real treat to serve fish and chips to the guests. I know some people will laugh at this, but I think everyone has probably been to a wedding where they just had silly little bits of food, and they ended up hungry and stopping at the chippy on the way home. Well, we brought the chippy to the wedding!

It was very upmarket fish and chips, from a firm in Soho that has been in business for more than twenty years, and which has the reputation of the best fish and chips in London. And it fitted in perfectly with my traditional English theme, especially as the fish and chips were served in newspaper. Of course, nowadays the newspaper has to be lined, but it made it all look wonderfully old-fashioned.

Everyone was really surprised and delighted. By the time the food was served the guests were quite hungry, so they were all tucking in. We didn't have a formal seating plan, so everyone was free to mingle, and the food was carried round to the tables by waiters. Preston and I took time to go round and chat to everyone, it was just so nice seeing all the people we care about together at the same time. The room looked lovely, with candles everywhere, as well as the amazing red roses. While we were eating we had a jazz band playing. Although I'm vegetarian on the whole, I eat some fish, and the cod was really lovely. I hadn't eaten much during the day because of nerves, so I was ready for my fish and chips.

Dad, Preston and Matt – Preston's best man, and best friend from college – all made speeches. Dad welcomed everybody and said how proud he was of both his children, Gregg as well as me.

'I've always known Chantelle was something special,' he said, 'but today she has made me the proudest man in the world. Words cannot express how I feel. I am so very proud to be standing up here as her father and I wish the pair of them all the love and happiness in the world.'

I felt chuffed to bits hearing that.

Preston and Matt both made very funny speeches. Preston recited some funny poems and said, 'A prerequisite for being here today was to be a loved one, and we love everyone in this room' and he was absolutely right!

Even our wedding cake was really special. We didn't want an iced fruit cake with marzipan like most people have, so we ordered a chocolate cake from a firm called choccywoccydoodah, based in Brighton. It was beautiful, all made from chocolate, ivory-coloured and with red roses decorating it, to match the colour theme of the wedding. The people who made it were really great – I changed my mind about the design just a week before the wedding, but they were cool about it.

Having the *OK!* photographer there was really good, because he was unobtrusive, and just took pictures the way a wedding photographer would. At the same time, he's experienced on this kind of shoot, and I knew there would be some lovely pictures.

In the evening, we had the DJ Matt Maurice. Preston and I danced the first dance together, to Buddy Holly's 'Every Day'. Everyone said my dress looked really beautiful, twirling around. It was really heavy and, before long, I slipped my ivory shoes off and was barefoot underneath it – but you couldn't see, and nobody noticed.

At about 10 p.m. I changed out of it, because the weight was beginning to make my stomach hurt – and also because Preston had bought me a beautiful dress for the evening, a black silk sleeveless dress with one shoulder strap. I'd bought some Dior shoes to go with it, for £450 – the most money I have ever spent on a pair of shoes! But it was my wedding after all! They have high heels and are encrusted with diamanté. Preston also bought me an Alexander McQueen necklace, with skulls, and arms and ribcages – it sounds a bit gruesome but it's really cool, and it looked really nice with the dress.

Then there was a karaoke, which was brilliant fun. Preston was up there singing lots of times and everyone had a go. I sang a couple of times, doing a duet with Lucy, my new sister-in-law. We sang a rendition of 4 Non Blondes', 'What's Up', which didn't sound bad at all, though I say it myself! Preston and Dean sang 'Up on the Roof' together, which is Dean's favourite song, and afterwards Preston said he'd found a new backing singer!

Then Gregg and his friend had a go, singing 'Hey Jude'. It was a real laugh, and everyone had a great time. From the minute the music started, the dance floor was always full.

Mum tells me that after having a couple of cocktails at the beginning, she didn't drink any more alcohol.

'I wanted to remember every bit of it,' she said. 'I can have a drink any time, but I didn't want to wake up the next day and be unable to go over every little detail. It was just a perfect day.' And, funnily enough, 'Perfect Day' was what Preston sang as the last song.

It was about 12.30 p.m. when we finally went to bed. It had been a long day, but it was such a shame it was over. I loved every single minute. Nothing went wrong, everyone enjoyed themselves, and for us it was really special. At the end of the night, after everybody had gone, we looked at each other and both of us said we just couldn't believe what an amazing day it had been. It was exactly as we'd hoped. Now that we are married, I am ecstatically happy. If I could have dreamed up a perfect life, this would be it.

The next big thing on the agenda for us is to find a house. The trouble is, househunting takes a lot of time and commitment, and time is in short supply because we are both so busy. But next year we will definitely find somewhere. We're hoping to stay in the Brighton area, because we both love it.

We do plan to have babies one day – after all, we're married, and that's one of the reasons you get married! But we don't have any immediate plans: we want to enjoy ourselves just being together, maybe travelling a bit. I also

A Whole New World

Katie Price

Katie Price reveals all about her passionate and whirlwind romance with Peter Andre. After more than her fair share of heartbreak Katie has at last found true love and this time she knows it's for keeps. Physically and emotionally she has met her match and there have been some dramatic changes in her life as a result. She talks about how Peter proposed, why they kept her pregnancy with Junior a secret for five months, and she reveals what it felt like to be the celebrity bride of the decade.

But behind the fairy tale, Katie talks about her heartache over her son Harvey's continuing ill health and her own struggle to cope after the birth of her son, Junior. She talks, too, about how hard she has found it coming to terms with Pete's past relationships . . .

This is the one celebrity of the year that will give you the no holds barred truth from the woman who always speaks her mind.

'A real page-turner' *OK!*

'Intimate, riveting confessions . . . It's a full-on passionate love story' *Daily Mail*

'A truly compelling read . . . this latest look at her life makes for seriously juicy reading' *heat*

'Compulsive reading' *More*

'A revealing romp that you'll find hard to put down' *Star magazine*

arrow books

Angel

Katie Price

A sparkling and sexy tale of glamour modelling, romance and the treacherous promises of fame.

When Angel is discovered by a model agent, her life changes for ever. Young, beautiful and sexy, she seems destined for a successful career and, very quickly, the glitzy world of celebrity fame and riches becomes her new home.

But then she meets Mickey, the lead singer of a boy band, who is as irresistible as he is dangerous, and Angel realises that a rising star can just as quickly fall . . .

'The perfect sexy summer read' *heat*

'A page-turner . . . it is brilliant. Genuinely amusing and readable. This summer, every beach will be polka-dotted with its neon pink covers' *Evening Standard*

'The perfect post-modern fairy tale' *Glamour*

arrow books

Straight

Boy George

Boy George: singer, songwriter, theatre star, DJ, photographer, fashion designer, cultural icon.

Told with George's trademark biting wit, brutal honesty and sparkling insight, this book reveals the whole story, reappraising his rise to stardom and all the madness that followed. He talks about his solo singing career, his initiation in the dance music scene, and his role as the driving force behind theatrical sensation Taboo. George also discusses the achievement of the apparently factious Culture Club.

It is only now, many years on from the glittering, glossy eighties, that George makes an insightful and often hilarious assessment of the impact of that extraordinary era.

Boy George has gone far from those days of excess and addiction.

This is his story.

'communicates and expresses the energy of an intelligent anarchist holding an anti-bullshit device . . .' *Guardian*

'painfully tender . . . I loved it' *Daily Telegraph*

''The best book I've read in a long while . . . it made me howl with laughter and burst into tears' Paul O'Grady

'Bitchy, opinionated and fabulously indiscreet' *Q*

arrow books

Frank Skinner

Frank Skinner

The Best Selling Autobiography

Frank Skinner is undoubtedly one of the funniest and most successful comedians appearing on British screens.

Born Chris Collins in 1957 he grew up in the West Midlands where he inherited his father's passion for football, a West Bromich Albion supporter, along with a liking for alcohol. Expelled from school at 16 Frank held various jobs later going on to gain an MA in English Literature. Nurturing a serious drink problem from the age of fourteen, Frank eventually turned to Catholicism in 1987 and hasn't had a drink since.

He performed his first stand up gig in December 1987. His first television appearance in 1988 met with fits of laughter from the audience and 131 complaints, including one from cabinet-minister Edwina Currie. He met fellow comedian David Baddiel in 1990 and the two went on to share a flat throughout the early 90's and to create the hit TV series *Fantasy Football League*.

Winner of the prestigious Perrier Award at the Edinburgh Festival, Skinner's is a unique mixture of laddish and philosophical humour.

Here, for the first time, Frank candidly tells us of the highs and lows of his fascinating life and career.

arrow books

The Armstrongs' A-Z Guide to Life

John and Ann Armstrong

The BBC created a fantastically cult television series when they filmed the daily operations of John and Ann's double glazing firm U-Fit, the third largest in Coventry. It was here we were first introduced to John's misanthropic musings and no-nonsense attitude to management and his wife Ann's doting loyalty.

Now their individual and highly entertaining personalities have been brought to the page, as they ruminate on various aspects of life from asbos to Buddhism, and Chekov to Maltesers.

The Armstrongs' A-Z Guide to Life will take you from all you can eat buffets to zero tolerance via everything in between.

arrow books

Elvis by the Presleys

Twenty eight years after his death, Elvis Presley remains one of the world's most beloved and iconic figures. There has been an impressive array of bestselling Elvis books over the years, but there has never been a book like this. Now, for the first time, Elvis, the man, husband father and artist, is remembered intimately and honestly by his ex wife Priscilla, daughter Lisa Marie and other close family members.

Including deeply personal documents and previously unseen family photographs, this sensational book also features new interviews with family and friends.

From personal diary entries to unearthed artefacts, *Elvis by the Presleys* is a publishing phenomenon and comes closer than any other book in revealing the private dreams and truths of the extraordinary and complex man, who became the king of Rock and Roll.

'Genuinely moving' *Saturday Times*

arrow books

What if I Had Never Tried It

Valentino Rossi

First GP win aged 17. First world title at 18. First 500 class win at 21. First MotoGP win at 22. Current MotoGP World Champion. Living Legend.

Valentino Rossi is the greatest motorcyclist on earth. Wherever he goes, legions of fans follow him, in awe of his professionalism and skill on the track, and his style and charisma off it.

On the bike: Five World Championship wins. Top three ranking in the World Championship for nine years in a row. Wins on a Honda and wins on a Yamaha.

Off the bike: Super-cool, scorchingly engaging, unnervingly rebellious, with pop-star fame and charm.

Valentino Rossi: Brilliant, talented, always relaxed, and very, very fast.

'While the autobiography details everything you could want to know about him and his career, you don't need to be a bike fan to enjoy it. It is truly inspiring stuff' – *The Sun*

arrow books

Back from the Brink

Paul McGrath

Paul McGrath is Ireland's best loved sportsman and also its least understood. An iconic football presence during a professional career stretching over 14 years, he played for his country in the European Championship finals of 1988 and the World Cup finals of 1990 and 1994. But, behind the implied glamour of life in the employ of great English clubs like Manchester United and Aston Villa, McGrath wrestled with a range of destructive emotions that made his success in the game little short of miraculous.

That story has until now never been told. It is a story that runs from a hard, hidden childhood spent in Dublin's orphanages all the way to the pain of two marriage break-ups, his all-too public struggle with alcoholism, and the surreal highs and calamitous lows of a life lived habitually on the edge of chaos.

It is not just a football story. It is an extraordinary human story.

'Laceratingly honest . . . remarkably unflinching' *Mail on Sunday*

'Gripping [and] unflinching . . . His story is as complex as it is moving, as vulnerable as it is brutal' *Guardian*

arrow books

21st Century Star Signs

Babs Kirby

Ever wondered how best to win round a stubborn colleague, or why it is you can never settle for just one partner? Babs Kirby's *21st Century Star Signs* will tell you everything you ever wanted to know about you, your lover, father, daughter, boss and even today's A-list celebrities, in this, the most modern, in-depth astrological portrait for the 21st century.

Taking up where the massive bestseller Linda Goodman's *Sun Signs* left off, Babs takes a completely contemporary, zeitgeisty approach that's compassionate, intelligent and, above all, revealing. 21st Century Star Signs reflects and embraces today's sensibilities and values looking at the way we function in sexual relationships – whether they're heterosexual, metrosexual, gay (or otherwise-), in work – with all it's ever-changing technologies and opportunities and in our homelife in which single parents, serial monogomists and stay-at-home fathers are now the norm.

A chapter is dedicated to each sign, giving an in-depth portrait which will reveal every aspect of the sign including both positive and negative aspects, bringing hidden motivations, sexual proclivities and characteristics to the fore and showing how different signs will thrive under certain circumstance, how to nurture one's positive influences and how best to recognise, relate to and deal with other signs – with all their strengths and weaknesses.

arrow books

THE POWER OF READING

Visit the Random House website and get connected with information on all our books and authors

EXTRACTS from our recently published books and selected backlist titles

COMPETITIONS AND PRIZE DRAWS Win signed books, audiobooks and more

AUTHOR EVENTS Find out which of our authors are on tour and where you can meet them

LATEST NEWS on bestsellers, awards and new publications

MINISITES with exclusive special features dedicated to our authors and their titles

READING GROUPS Reading guides, special features and all the information you need for your reading group

LISTEN to extracts from the latest audiobook publications

WATCH video clips of interviews and readings with our authors

RANDOM HOUSE INFORMATION including advice for writers, job vacancies and all your general queries answered

Come home to Random House

www.randomhouse.co.uk